TAKING EVERY THOUGHT CAPTIVE

MEN OF VALOR SERIES

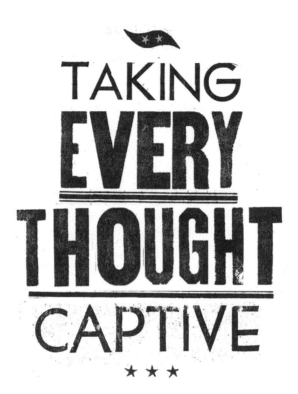

TAKING EVERY THOUGHT CAPTIVE

mark r. laaser

BEACON HILL PRESS
OF KANSAS CITY

Copyright 2011 by Mark R. Laaser and Beacon Hill Press of Kansas City

ISBN 978-0-8341-2741-8

Printed in the
United States of America

Cover Design: Brandon Hill
Interior Design: Sharon Page

Library of Congress Cataloging-in-Publication Data

Laaser, Mark R.
    Taking every thought captive / Mark R. Laaser.
        p. cm.
    Includes bibliographical references (p.   ).
    ISBN 978-0-8341-2741-8 (pbk.)
    1. Thought and thinking—Religious aspects—Christianity. 2. Spiritual life—Christianity. I. Title.
    BV4598.4.L33 2011
    248.4—dc23

                                                                    2011024834

10 9 8 7 6 5 4 3 2

CONTENTS

ACKNOWLEDGMENTS

No one really writes a book alone. There are those who have contributed ideas, those who have reviewed ideas and content, and those who support through encouragement and prayer. That has certainly been the case for me.

First and foremost is the person who has contributed, reviewed, encouraged, and prayed the most—my wife, Debbie. We have been married for thirty-eight years. During that time she has gone through the good times and the bad and never stopped being my number one friend, companion, and soul mate. She is often way ahead of me emotionally and spiritually. She has been the main way that God has demonstrated his grace to me. It has been our ministry together helping couples survive the crisis of infidelity that has shaped and formed many of the ideas in this book series. To Debbie, I can never say thank you enough.

A great deal of inspiration has come through my work with men who struggle with infidelity and sex addiction. Each and every one of the hundreds I have worked with has taught me something. There is a smaller number who really helped shape the material in this book. Anonymity issues prevent me from recognizing them more publicly.

Several men introduced me to certain concepts in these books. I am honored to say that they are colleagues and friends. Chris Charleton first pointed me to the powerful example of the story of Nehemiah and how it reveals to us a plan for accountability. Eli Machen is a superb teacher on many subjects, and his ideas on vision are what originally influenced me about it. More recently, Greg Miller has been helping me more fully understand the value of our needing a team of people to help us heal. To all of these men I say, "Thank you very much!"

To the wonderful family of people at Beacon Hill Press of Kansas City, thank you for your confidence, faith, and trust in me. Eric Bryant originally approached me about this series, and Bonnie Perry has nurtured it along.

And in all things to God be the glory. There are times for all Christian writers, I think, when they try to simply sit at the computer, quiet their spirits, and invite God to give them insight and inspiration. I pray that all readers of these books will open themselves to this quiet place and will allow God to speak to them directly through the imperfect words, thoughts, and ideas of this series. I could not put any book out there if I did not think that God was in charge of the process.

—Mark R. Laaser
January 2011

INTRODUCTION
WELCOME TO THE JOURNEY

We demolish arguments and every pretension that sets itself up against the knowledge of God, and we take captive every thought to make it obedient to Christ (2 Cor. 10:5).

Do not conform any longer to the pattern of this world, but be transformed by the renewing of your mind. Then you will be able to test and approve what God's will is— his good, pleasing and perfect will (Rom. 12:2).

The preceding words of Paul are two verses from different letters. They are short and powerful and also introduce you to the main theme of this book. I want to teach you that they are just as relevant to our time as they were to Paul's world in the first century. Mainly, I want to teach you how to take your thoughts captive, making them obedient to Christ, and so transform your mind.

This is a bold task and I do not take it lightly. I feel so strongly about it because taking your thoughts captive is essential in today's world. To say we are swimming in a sea of immoral behaviors and messages would be to put it mildly. We are experiencing the same kind of moral crisis that has historically led to the decline of countless cultures. The world Paul wrote to in the first century was one such declining culture. In the first chapter of Romans, Paul does not hold back in describing the sexual immorality of that time. Then he goes on to describe people of the Roman world:

> Furthermore, since they did not think it worthwhile to retain the knowledge of God, he gave them over to a depraved mind, to do what ought not to be done. They have become filled with every kind of wickedness, evil, greed and depravity. They are full of envy, murder, strife, deceit and malice. They are gossips, slanderers, God-haters, insolent, arrogant and boastful; they invent ways of doing evil; they disobey their parents; they are senseless, faithless, heartless, ruthless. Although they know God's righteous decree that those who do such things deserve death, they not only continue to do these very things but also approve of those who practice them. (Rom. 1:28-32)

The moral condition of the Roman world is why later in the book of Romans (12:2) Paul teaches that people should not conform to the ways of this kind of world but that they should transform their mind. The Greek word *nous*, which Paul uses here, is generally translated as "mind" but can also mean "intellect," "will," or "reason." In New Testament times, the mind was also thought to be the center of moral thinking. Paul is teaching that the mind can be either evil, according to the ways of the world, or good, as it is transformed according to God's will.

To be good we will need our will, reasoning, and intellect. In Hebrew, there is no word for mind because another part of the body, the heart, was thought to possess the qualities of what we now know as the brain. So the heart can be pure, holy, courageous, clean, and stubborn, as well as evil or good. We still to this day use the word "heart" to describe character qualities, such as, "He really has a good heart." The Bible, in fact, uses the word "heart" 570 times to refer to our mind and our character. The psalmist uses the word "heart" to show that a person can be perverse: "Men of perverse heart shall be far from me; I will have nothing to do with evil" (Ps. 101:4).

Today we know that our brain is where all the functions and qualities of the mind or heart take place. The brain reasons, remembers, plans, and decides. It can have powerful emotions like anger, sadness, fear, and anxiety. Thoughts all take place in the brain. In order to know how to take thoughts captive and how to transform our mind, we will need to know how to do so in the brain. The good news is that new scientific research shows that this is not only a spiritual phenomenon but an actual anatomical one as well. In chapter 3 I will teach you about all of this.

What would Paul have to say about our current world? Could the descriptions of Rom. 1 accurately depict moral conditions today? Think about the lust and greed that are regular influences on our lives. Ask yourself to count from the time you get up to the time you go to bed how many immoral messages you are bombarded with. Start with TV, movies, music, and magazines, but don't forget the conversations that take place all around you and the images that are being demonstrated by how people dress (even at church). Add to your list any recent statistics you have read or heard about pornography use, infidelity, divorce, STDs, or abortion. Then factor in the news about financial corruption, murder, and random acts of unkindness. Whatever you come up with as you read this will be more current than the dismal statistics I could write about here. Suffice it to say that just like in Paul's time, our minds, hearts, and brains cannot conform to this kind of world.

There is one similarity and one huge difference between our world and Paul's. In his day, the Roman Empire had managed to create a relatively peaceful time. There were no major wars or conquests going on. Travel and communication were readily available to all, which contributed to the spread of the gospel. In God's timing, Paul and the other disciples were able to travel and bring the message of Christ to countless cultures and peoples. Despite our wars against terrorism around the world, our time is also relatively free of the kind of conflict that prevents travel. Travel is obviously faster and more accessible to all of us than it was back then.

The biggest difference today is the forms of communication that are available, mainly through the Internet, with computers and smart phones. I remember how wonderful it was back in the fifties to get fifteen minutes of national news on one of only three TV channels. Think of the differences today. I remember what it was like to send a letter. I could never have imagined staying in touch with hundreds of people through social networking when I was a young adult. Back then you had to go to a casino in Las Vegas to gamble, there was no fast food, and to look at pornography you had to get past your inhibitions to find it in a drugstore or a seedy bookstore. Today, all of this is available either through the Internet or no more than a five-minute drive from most of our houses.

All of this has brought an explosion of pornography and gambling, and we are as a whole a more obese group of people than we have ever been. Given the fact that temptation is only a click away, there has never been a more difficult time to resist temptations of all kinds. Those of you who never imagined having an affair were possibly surprised to be contacted by your old high school girlfriend on Facebook. Some of you who thought your habit of looking at pornography ended when you got married have been surprised by how easy it is to get hooked by all the available free material. My examples are endless.

Where does all this instant temptation take us? The answer is to decisions that must be made in our hearts or minds. Every temptation begins with a thought. Therefore, if we are going to make healthy decisions, avoid temptation and the sin it leads to, we had better learn to control our thought life. Paul knew it and tells us to take every thought captive and make it obedient to Christ.

Have you ever been confused by what this means? In this book, I want to teach what it means and give you some practical ways to do it. I feel strongly about this because over the years I have often heard well-meaning, but ineffective advice about how to do so. Throughout this book I will be teaching you about methods that work and methods that don't. As you read, I will be challenging you in each chapter to ask yourself some basic questions in order to help you digest and understand the material.

If you have read my book in this series on accountability, *The 7 Principles of Highly Accountable Men,* you will know that it could be important to read this book with a group of other people, men or women. Challenge yourself to take the questions and insights seriously and also challenge each other to practice them. Encourage yourself and others that it is possible to lead a life that is free of evil thoughts. Wouldn't it be great to go through life not being challenged by thoughts that you believed you couldn't control?

For years I believed I couldn't control my thoughts. I started looking at pornography when I was eleven years old, and the pattern of lustful thoughts that it created over the next twenty-five years led me into escalating sexually sinful activity. I was out of control and had an addiction. At age thirty-seven, my friends and family staged an intervention. I agreed to go to a treatment center where I got "sober" for the first time in my life. I have been so for the last twenty-three years. During that time I have had to learn how to control my lustful thoughts and temptations. What follows in this book is all that I've learned from my own experiences and the experiences of thousands of men I've worked with. While my learning has been primarily about sexual lust, the principles I want to teach you can apply to any sinful or unwanted thoughts.

Please read on with diligence, courage, and patience. The journey is well worth it.

1
THE BEHAVIORAL APPROACH

In this chapter I want to teach you some things you might do to guard against unwanted thoughts before they even happen. Most of these strategies I first learned from my recovery in twelve-step programs for addiction. Back in 1987, there were very few groups for sex addiction, so I was told to go to Alcoholics Anonymous (AA) meetings, even though I'm not alcoholic. That was one of the best things that has ever happened to me because AA is so rich in wisdom about accountability and what really works. Alcoholics Anonymous has a lot to say about unwanted thoughts, which it calls "stinking thinking."[1] An alcoholic must learn what to do with the thought or temptation of drinking. I believe that all of us can use some of the twelve-step principles whether or not we experience an addiction.

I want to emphasize that these behavioral approaches to taking thoughts captive are only the first step. Behavioral solutions are only short-term strategies, not long-term solutions. Eventually, I want to teach you those longer-term solutions, but the following may help you get started.

Avoiding Triggers

A trigger is stimulus that causes a thought. If you avoid the trigger, you therefore avoid the thought. The first step to use this strategy is to understand what a trigger is and what particular triggers you struggle with. Basically a trigger is anything that goes from your five senses to your brain. You hear them, see them, smell them, taste them, or physically feel them. The other day someone told me that one of the local electronic stores was having a sale. I heard this and immediately started thinking about that new computer I "need" to buy but can't afford. My thought was of the computer. To avoid it would have required not talking to my friend, or, as part of my accountability program, to have asked him to never mention anything to me about electronics sales.

One of the men I am working with told me today that he was watching a football game and an ad for lingerie came on. It triggered a thought of sexuality in his brain, and the temptation was to go and find more explicit pictures of women on the Internet. To avoid this kind of trigger, he would need to not watch the game or, at least, not watch any of the commercials. Many people tell me they can be at a mall and the sight of attractive people triggers sexual longing. To avoid this, they would either have to avoid going to the mall or, while there, look down or look away. One common strategy for avoiding visual triggers is to "bounce" your eyes. That means if you see something that is visually stimulating, you must bounce your head or your eyes away from it. The men I work with who struggle with sexual thoughts may seek to avoid places where people are more provocatively dressed, like a beach or swimming pool. Members of Gamblers Anonymous routinely get rid of all credit cards and only carry a small amount of cash in their wallets.

Even in Old Testament times the writer of Proverbs warns about avoiding the trigger of an adulteress: "Now then, my sons, listen to me; do not turn aside from what I say. Keep to a path far from her, do not go near the door of her house, lest you give your best strength to others and your years to one who is cruel" (5:7-9).

One of the most common sexual triggers today comes from TV, magazines, or the Internet. If these kinds of triggers are problems for you, you may need to avoid reading magazines, watching TV, or surfing the Internet.

If thoughts of eating food are your problem, you may be triggered by the sight or taste of food. If I'm in the mall and walk by the cinemas and smell the popcorn, I'm going to want to eat popcorn because the thought of it is in my head. While in the mall, the perfume section of the department store may trigger me into thoughts of an old girlfriend. Driving down the highway I may see the billboard for the lottery jackpot and my thoughts turn to gambling. Are you getting the idea?

Triggers are always based on our life experience. My popcorn trigger is based on years of pleasant times at the movies, all associated with eating popcorn. Food triggers are usually associated with pleasant times in the past, such as times spent with family or connecting with friends. Sexual triggers can be associated with past sexual experiences. Gambling triggers are always associated with that time you actually won a jack-pot. For alcoholics, times of drinking are sometimes associated with fellowship. Remember the TV series *Cheers*? It was a bar and the place "where everybody knows your name."[2]

Let's be realistic; if we are to avoid all triggers, we would have to lead the life of a monk or hermit. This is not very realistic, and I believe my wife would object to that. So avoidance is not the final solution. In the early stages of learning how to take every thought captive, however, there will be obvious stimuli that we may choose to aggressively avoid.

⊕ KEY POINT

Triggers are stimuli that create unwanted thoughts.

⊕ KEY QUESTIONS

- What stimuli do you readily notice? What things do you hear, see, feel, taste, or touch that trigger sinful thoughts in your brain? Remember, everyone is different, so don't be afraid to claim things that you fear would not trigger anyone else.

- Whatever triggers you today, can you recall some association you have with it in past exciting or pleasant events?

- What might you realistically avoid today so as not to be triggered?

- Would you be willing to be accountable about those triggers?

As I said, you can't avoid all triggers forever. They happen. One of my sayings is, "Triggers are the gift that keeps on giving." So they happen, now what do we do?

The Three-Second Rule

I made a covenant with my eyes not to look lustfully at a girl (Job 31:1). Another AA strategy is the three-second rule, which is a basic reminder that if we allow a thought in our brain for longer than three seconds, it becomes a preoccupation or obsession. One of my colleagues says that we may not even have that long, and it is probably more like three-tenths of a second. Whatever is true, we should realize that when an unwanted, selfish, or lustful thought enters our brain, it is probably because of some stimulus, which we should at that point remove ourselves from. So if something on TV is triggering us, we should turn off the TV. If an attractive person triggers lustful thoughts, we should probably figure out a way to politely walk away from him or her. If we are involved in a conversation where the subject matter is a trigger, we might even be honest about it and ask to change the subject.

One of the men I am working with, for example, recently told me that one of his friends was continually sending him information on Web sites that had sexual content on them. At the risk of his friendship, he directly asked the friend to not send him those emails any longer.

The mantra of this approach can be, "Look away, walk away, turn away, get away, or take a time-out." Remember, the most important thing is taking every thought captive, not making sure everyone understands what you are doing.

⊛ KEY POINT

Once we have a thought, we should try to remove ourselves as quickly as possible from whatever trigger caused it in the first place.

⊛ KEY QUESTION

- Would you be willing to make a covenant with someone and/or your accountability network that you will do what is necessary when a thought is triggered to not let it become a preoccupation or obsession?

Think Through the Drink

Another classic AA strategy is to take a thought captive and imagine the eventual damage that thought might cause in your life. So if an alcoholic is tempted to drink, he or she is asked to remember what has usually happened when he or she drinks. The person is to "think through the drink." He or she is encouraged to imagine the worst possible scenario. If a person is tempted to drink and then to drive home, he or she would be asked to imagine getting into an accident and being killed or killing someone else, or to imagine being arrested and losing his or her driver's license. People who have lustful thoughts and fantasize about an affair should think through the consequences of divorce, family breakups, acquiring a sexually transmitted disease, or losing their jobs. Gamblers would see themselves losing until they have lost all of their money and are bankrupt. Overeaters think through the medical consequences of obesity and even death.

Most people have enough life experience with the results of their thoughts to know how awful they can be, making it not hard to imagine future consequences. Unfortunately for some who struggle with addiction, being aware of consequences is not enough to get them to stop. This dynamic can, in fact, be part of what defines addiction.

Once basic sobriety is achieved, however, this strategy can be effective in reminding you to not get started again.

● KEY POINT

Consequences of past behavior can be used as a deterrent in the future.

● KEY QUESTIONS

- What have been past consequences of your thoughts? Make as complete a list of those as possible.

- Would you be willing to share that list with someone?

● KEY ASSIGNMENT

Write a letter to yourself as if you had acted out again or had lustful thoughts. Remind yourself in the letter of what the consequences of your thoughts and behaviors would be. Then fold the letter and put it in your wallet. Read as necessary.

Learning to Make Phone Calls

In my book *The 7 Principles of Highly Accountable Men*, I teach about the principles that will keep people accountable to their vision of the future.[3] One of the disciplines that is a part of those seven principles is making phone calls to people in an accountability group. What this means in the simplest of terms is that the second an intrusive thought enters your brain, you pick up the phone and call someone to whom you are accountable.

Remember that this assumes you have a group of people who know your story enough to know you have such thoughts. You will need to take the time to share your story with others. You will also need to ask others for permission to call when you need to. Most people who are in accountability networks are willing because they need to make calls themselves. It is most usual, therefore, for you to also receive calls if you participate in a group.

Now, the challenge is that with many temptations and thoughts, there are parallel thoughts such as, "You don't really want to make this call. It would be so much more fun and much less hassle to have your thought and continue your behavior."

What this means is that if you wait until temptation happens, it will usually be too late.

My advice is that you get in the habit of making calls every day, whether or not you need to. Most of the time you may simply check in and talk about superficial matters. Then, when you need to call about impure thoughts, you will be in the calling habit. You have traded bad thoughts for good thoughts. You will know that others are expecting your calls and may call you if they don't regularly hear from you.

Often intrusive, unwanted, and obsessive thoughts produce a trance-like state in the brain. The habit of making calls will be a way to break out of that trance. Many people tell me that simply listening to someone else's voicemail message is enough to break them out of the unwanted pattern. In this way, the habit of making and receiving calls is like programming your brain to automatically make calls. It is a very real way to take thoughts captive.

● KEY POINT

Making phone calls is a matter of discipline and practice. Remember that the more calls you make a routine, the more calls you will make. There is nothing like talking to someone else to stop unwanted patterns of thought.

● KEY QUESTIONS

- How are you at making calls in general? Some people have never been comfortable with it and, therefore, practice for them will be a more gradual process.

- Are you open to receiving calls?

- Would you be willing to ask others if you can call them?

● KEY ASSIGNMENT

Put the numbers of the people you are regularly going to call in the speed dial program of your cell phone, that way they are only one button away from helping you take thoughts captive.

Distracting Yourself

Over the years I have talked to countless people who tell me when they have unwanted thoughts, they do something to distract themselves. Basically this means they try to switch to other thoughts that are healthy. Doing this can also be a matter of training your mind. Some tell me they switch to memorized scripture, the words of hymns or songs, or messages they create for themselves.

Of course, some of this can depend on what kind of problem you are dealing with. For example, a man who is struggling with thoughts of an affair may try to switch to thoughts of his wife, kids, or family. Food addicts put pictures of very fit people on their refrigerators to help them switch to their vision of losing weight. A workaholic may try to switch to thoughts of vacations or recreational activities. Do you get the idea?

I will have much more to teach about this later, but for now remember that seeking to distract yourself may lead to frustration because it doesn't always work. This strategy, like everything else in this chapter, is only one weapon in your arsenal for taking thoughts captive.

● KEY POINT

Distracting yourself from unwanted thoughts is very much a matter of practice, some of which includes knowing not to get too frustrated when this strategy doesn't always work.

● KEY QUESTIONS

- Do you have scripture, words of music, or other messages memorized?

- If not, would you be willing to?

This is chapter 1 of the book. The strategies are more immediate and can be practiced right away. Don't lose heart when they don't always work or don't work forever. There are strategies ahead that may rid you of all unwanted thoughts, making those in this chapter unnecessary.

2

USING MEDITATION TO TAKE THOUGHTS CAPTIVE

In my accountability, I try to be honest, but this has not always been the case. In my old life, my wife would often ask me what I was thinking or feeling and I would either say, "Nothing," or make up something I believed would make her feel better. I was not willing to tell her my true thoughts because in some cases I was afraid they might hurt her or, in others, might make her think I was weird or awful. I did not know that taking thoughts captive might involve being honest about the ones I have.

Today, I try to be honest, though it is still not easy some-times. I admit that so that you will understand it is hard for me to be honest now and admit the following. I am not an expert on meditation. I write this chapter because I believe in how incredibly powerful it is. I have seen the benefit of it in countless lives. A part of my weakness in this area is due to my history. I was raised in an Evangelical Protestant tradition that, in my opinion, never taught about meditation. It was not until graduate school when I studied world religions that I was introduced to it, and I rejected meditation because I rejected those religions. What I didn't realize is that meditation is not the exclusive province of Buddhism or Hinduism, among others, but that it is a very real part of the Christian tradition. Protestants still don't always like talking about it because there is a fear that others might be confused about the sincerity of their beliefs. There are other words or phrases used to describe meditation, such as "reflection" or "quiet time," that you may be more comfortable with.

There is another factor in my challenge with meditation. It is called attention deficit disorder (ADD), and it means my brain is very easily distracted by thoughts. I have been very skeptical that I could focus on anything long enough to practice meditation. Whether or not you have any attention issues, you may also think that you can't tolerate sitting quietly and reflecting. The truth is that meditation is a discipline and it does take practice. You will gradually build an ability to do it.

Meditating can be a very powerful tool in taking every thought captive. When our brains are calm and we are more focused, it is less likely that obtrusive thoughts can find their way in. Though I am no expert, there are a number of ways to meditate that might get you started.

A Place of Your Own

My wife, Debbie, believes it is very important to have a physical space in your home where you can be alone. She calls it a POYO, or a place of your own. It can be an entire room, like your office or study, or it might simply be a special chair that only you sit in.

✪ KEY POINT

Find, establish, and declare to all who live with you what and where your POYO is.

Music

Most of us like to listen to music. My guess is that you already know what type of music puts you in a quiet and reflective mood, which is inherently meditative. My suggestion is that you experiment with what works. I don't think I need to give you suggestions about how to obtain or find music. I am old-fashioned and like CDs, but I know these days that most music is acquired online in one of a variety of ways.

According to research on the effects of music on the brain, in general, classical music produces a very calming effect, while rock music produces a very negative effect. Any music, including Christian, that has a heavy drum or guitar beat, is rather awful for the brain. That kind of music often creates excitement through adrenaline, which causes a very active response. While it may make us feel good, it is not quieting. I believe that many churches turn to this kind of feel-good music to attract people. There can be no doubt, however, that quieter music produces a more meditative and therefore more worshipful feeling. I can hear the responses from many music ministers: "Yes, but that kind of music is old, moldy, and boring." We may not use it to stay awake during Sunday services, but we could use it as part of our regular spiritual discipline of meditation.

Wherever you find music, I would encourage you to take a few minutes every day to just sit quietly and listen to it.

● KEY POINT

Certain types of music can produce a meditative state.

● KEY QUESTIONS

- Do you like listening to music?

- What type of music causes you to be reflective?

- What type causes you to be more active?

- Would you be willing to listen to music every day?

Prayer

Am I preaching to the choir about prayer? My guess is that the average reader of this book already knows about the importance of prayer. My experience is that most of us who do pray are rather quick about it and say prayers on the go. We pray when something comes up, someone asks us to pray for him or her, or before we begin a meal. None of those are bad, but they are rarely reflective.

Reflective prayer is quiet prayer. It is sitting still and talking to God. It may not be very organized, but it is thoughtful and deliberate. It may include periods of silence when we ask God to speak to us. It is quieting and allows God long enough to do so.

You might get into the discipline of prayer by reading a book of prayers. There are some really good ones out there, including some classics by the early church leaders. Have you ever read the prayers of Augustine of Hippo or of Thomas Aquinas, for example? Some of the great mystics of the church knew that it was prayer that brought their mystical awareness of the presence of God.

Another way to start a discipline of prayer is a strategy that someone taught me years ago. He said to keep a notebook with me and write down every time a person asked me to pray for him or her. Then, he said, at the end of the day, add to this list any person(s) you would like to pray for. Finally, simply read the list. The act of reading the list is really a form of prayer. Remember that not all prayer is poetic or dramatic; it is usually very simple.

A famous preacher I once heard introduced me to another strategy for prayer. He said that every day he writes down his prayers on his computer. He keeps an ongoing file of his prayers, including who and what he is praying for. Then he said he often goes back several years and reads those prayers again. Doing so amazed him because it allowed him to see how God had answered those prayers.

The discipline of listening to music can be combined with the discipline of prayer. There is definitely some music that is more conducive to praying.

✹ KEY POINT

Prayer is essential to meditation, quieting your mind, taking every thought captive, and asking God for help.

✹ KEY QUESTIONS

• What has been your experience with prayer?

• Have you ever prayed by yourself or only with others?

• Have you ever read a book of prayers?

• Who are you praying for today? Make a list.

Lectio Divina

Since my own Evangelical Protestant tradition was so devoid of anything meditative, I have searched in earlier church traditions for direction on how to meditate in a Christ-centered, biblically based manner. It has been through my Roman Catholic brothers that I found a system of contemplation and meditation that I know really works. It is called the *lectio divina*. How is your Latin? It simply means "divine reading" and is a formula for reading Scripture and allowing God to work in your life through it. It is thought that Benedict of Nursia, the founder of the Benedictine monastic order, first taught this method to the monks. Pope Gregory I made it more widely known. All of this was in the fourth and fifth centuries.

As with everything we have been talking about in this chapter, there is first a way to prepare for a divine reading:

- First, choose the scriptures you wish to pray. There is no set amount. A complete word picture is best, but single verses can also work really well. You may already be involved in an organized Bible study through church, but if not, you may want to find a program that allows you to read through the Bible in a systematic way. Whatever you choose, it is between you and God.

- Go to your POYO and get comfortable. Think about becoming attentive. Don't force it; just suggest attentiveness to yourself. Focus on your breathing; be aware of the rhythm of it, in and out. The Hebrew word *ruach* can mean both "breath" and "spirit." This correctly establishes the fact that concentrating on your breathing can help you be in touch with your spirit. Some people like to start with a word or phrase that allows them to go to a deeper place. Given the power of words or phrases, try saying, "Breath on me, breath of God; fill me with life anew." A friend of mine uses a saying that has seven syllables (seven is a well-known and important number in meditation): "Abba [the Aramaic word for father or dad], I belong to you."

Now, the divine reading of Scripture has four phases. Try to let these flow, and if you get distracted, gently allow yourself to come back to the phase you're in.

- Phase One—*Lectio* (Reading). Turn to the text you have chosen and read it slowly, gently, out loud. Try to listen to the "still small voice" (1 Kings 19:12, KJV) of a particular word or phrase that is saying, "I have something to teach you today."

- Phase Two—*Meditatio* (Meditation). Take this word or phrase into yourself and slowly repeat it to yourself. Ask how this relates to your inner world of anxieties, concerns, memories, and ideas. Let your imagination engage the text and see if any images come to mind. These images may be messages or invitations from God to talk to him.

- Phase Three—*Oratio* (Prayer). What is God saying to me and what do I say to God through this text? Tell God what is on your heart. Imagine yourself having a conversation with God as you would with a friend. Ask God to bless and transform the thoughts and images that his Word has awakened in you.

- Phase Four—*Contemplatio* (Contemplation). Try to be still and let God work through your mind and heart. Try to let go of words and images. Be silent, rest, and receive.

I know if you're like me, this is a tall order and you might even be thinking that this is for pastors, priests, or monks, but not me. Let me suggest that you start with several very basic scriptures:

- Silence. "Be still, and know that I am God" (Ps. 46:10).

- Listen. "Each new generation will listen and learn to worship the LORD their God with fear and trembling" (Deut. 31:13, CEV).

- Dwell. "One thing I ask of the LORD, . . . that I may dwell in the house of the LORD all the days of my life" (Ps. 27:4).
- Abide. "Abide in me as I abide in you. . . . If you abide in me, and my words abide in you" (John 15:4, 7, NRSV).

You may be very surprised at how God really speaks to you through this spiritual discipline of prayer and Bible study. I have men that I work with who swear that since they have been doing the *lectio divina*, their sinful thought life has almost disappeared. What a weapon in your fight to take every thought captive.

⊛ KEY ASSIGNMENT

- Make a list of scriptures you already have memorized or know really well. Don't be ashamed or embarrassed if you don't really know too many.
- Ask a friend to share some verses or stories with you, particularly if you are rather new to Bible study.
- Finally, ask a friend to call you every day for a week and ask if you are focused on one verse or story today.

Journaling

This strategy is one I know is tough. It involves spending time every day writing your thoughts, concerns, worries, anxieties, prayers, and spiritual reflections (like from the *lectio divina*) down on paper, *longhand*. No computers allowed. "Why longhand?" you are asking. It is because writing something out has an ability to access the more reflective part of your brain. It really does.

This is a practice that has been around since the invention of paper. Go to any substantial bookstore and you'll find a section of very nice journals to buy. Many people do this. The historical record of many great leaders is often found in the journals they kept. In more modern times, since the advent of computers, some of us have almost forgotten how to write in longhand. (When is the last time you received a handwritten letter?)

If you want to try this one, give yourself a personal assignment. As a pastoral counselor, I often give my clients assignments. Sometimes it is to write letters that might never be sent to people about all the feelings you have for them. Another way to start is simply to sit down and write out the events of your day and your reactions to them. At a deeper level, start with one of the emotions that you have been experiencing a lot and reflect on it. As we will see later, journaling will be a process you can use to analyze the thoughts you are trying to capture. I am a big believer that by taking time to do this, you will go a long way toward eliminating those thoughts.

There are whole schools of thought devoted to the value of journaling in facilitating emotional and spiritual growth. There are some who have said that by journaling you won't have to see a counselor, therapist, psychologist, or pastor for help. Through the wisdom that is innate in all of us, with the power of the Holy Spirit, you can often come to the perfect solution for life's most difficult problems.

◉ KEY POINT

Journaling can produce a more reflective and meditative state in your mind. Remember, that place can help you take every thought captive.

◉ KEY QUESTIONS

- Have you ever tried journaling in the past?
- Do you own a journal that you have never used?
- How is your patience when it comes to writing long-hand?
- Have you ever had a reflective thought and said to yourself that you should write it down?

Repetition of Words

Please don't think that I have gone off some far-out deep end, but there is one final strategy I want to teach about. It involves repeating a word or series of words. Earlier I said that the seven-syllable phrase, "Abba, I belong to you," can be very powerful in reducing anxiety. Anxious thoughts are certainly ones that I have tried to take captive.

Repetition of words can be found in many of the world's religions, and that is often what scares some of us. By doing this, some fear that we will soon be taking trips to India to study with a guru. That is not at all the case. The truth is that this practice can be found in the earliest practices of Christianity. Roman Catholics, for example, might say the "Our Father" a number of times, which is really praying as Jesus taught us to pray. Catholics also have other repetitive prayers, such as the rosary. I find that since many of my Catholic friends have had to say these prayers from childhood, it is easy for them to have lost touch with their value. Since I never was forced to say them, I can come to the practice with an open mind and I achieve a very meditative state.

Have you ever had a saying, song, poem, or something you have made up yourself that you say over and over, perhaps especially in certain situations? I remember when one of our children who was facing a difficult task at school kept saying to himself the words from the famous story, "The Little Engine that Could": "I think I can, I think I can." Taking every thought captive might at times mean that you choose to say words over and over again to yourself instead of dwelling on the unwanted thoughts that you would otherwise have.

● KEY POINT

Repetitive words can be very rhythmic and take us to more meditative parts of our mind.

● KEY ASSIGNMENT

If this kind of work is really unfamiliar to you and you think it's worth a try, you may want to ask someone who does it often to give you some advice. Opening up a dialogue with a person from a different faith tradition might be very powerful.

I realize I have only scratched the surface of this topic. If meditating sounds really valuable to you in your battle to take every thought captive, find a pastor, spiritual director, or friend who is better at it to teach, coach, and keep you accountable.

3

TRANSFORMING THE BRAIN

So far we have considered how to guard your brain and how your brain can be meditative. If you are going to take every thought captive, your brain will need to cooperate with you in these strategies. Your brain isn't very cooperative, however, if it is suffering with mental health issues such as depression, anxiety disorder, manic depression, or attention deficit disorder (ADD). Your brain also won't be very cooperative if you have trained it through sinful choices to make those same choices again. Even if any of these or other problems aren't conditions you suffer with, I want to teach you about literally changing, physically transforming, your brain. Does that sound like a tall order?

Every so often new scientific discoveries confirm the truth of the Bible. Paul taught us that we should transform the mind in Rom. 7:15. We have generally assumed Paul was talking only about a spiritual transformation of the mind or brain. Today, scientists have been able to explore the workings of the brain in great detail. Whereas science once thought the brain was static and couldn't heal itself by reproducing new cells or cell connections, today's research has shown it can. This is exciting because it is no longer true that we must forever be prisoners of our genetics or medical histories. It is literally true that we can change our brains and change our lives.

Perhaps you've noticed the number of new books that address this topic. One of the first of this kind that was written from a truly scientific basis is by one of my good friends, Dr. Daniel Amen. His book was actually titled *Change Your Brain, Change Your Life*.[4] There are a variety of ways to actually see the functioning of the brain, and Dr. Amen was one of the first to look at the brain using a form of modern radiology called SPECT. Single Photon Emission Computed Tomography is a form that looks at the blood flow patterns of the brain or any other part of the body. Perhaps the most familiar is Functional Magnetic Resonance Imaging or FMRI. Since this is not a medical book, I am going to trust that if you are really interested in all of this radiology, you can get one of Dr. Amen's books or simply do your own research.

When the functioning of the brain is more accurately diagnosed by actually looking at it, very effective interventions and treatments can be used to restore the brain to health. This is not an uncommon approach. For a medical doctor to treat you for almost anything, he or she is going to want to get a picture of the part of your body being treated. A couple of years ago I went through a series of treatments for a heart problem. I'm glad to say that I don't have the problem today because my doctors were able to get very detailed pictures of my heart and thereby knew how to effectively treat it. Similarly, my dentist won't look into my mouth unless she has pictures of my teeth.

Historically, however, the most important part of the body, the brain, has been treated by simply asking a person certain questions about how he or she feels. How you feel depends on your perception of how you feel. Treatment, therefore, of mental health issues has been based on very educated guesses by psychiatrists, psychologists, and other mental health professionals. Guesses are guesses. Perhaps you have experienced how long it may take through trial and error to find the right treatment for any one of the mental health problems. I and many others today believe that the future of mental health treatment will largely depend on actually seeing the electrical and blood flow condition of the brain.

Those who struggle with anxiety, mood swings, who are chronically depressed, get stuck thinking about problems all the time, or have trouble focusing or concentrating may have even more trouble taking every thought captive. If any of these kinds of challenges are a concern for you, you may have experienced a great deal of shame because you can't seem to get certain negative thoughts out of your mind.

Take ADD, for example. Here are the symptoms of this condition:

- Short attention span
- Impulsivity
- Procrastination
- Disorganization
- Poor judgment
- Lack of empathy and insight

When you're trying to take every thought captive, imagine the additional hassle when you have these symptoms. We know, for example, from a number of studies that adults who have untreated ADD are twice as likely to have an addiction than the general population. In the men I directly work with who suffer with sexual addiction, half are likely to have ADD. Sex addicts are trying to take captive thoughts of sexual sin and get them out of their minds. Think about how much harder that is to do when you are impulsive and have poor judgment. Often an addict's spouse says that he or she doesn't understand the pain that's been caused, but that is because empathy is a problem for those with ADD.

People with depression are going to experience more intense feelings of sadness, discouragement, and even despair. Any attempt to take every thought captive that is not immediately successful will result in more negative feelings.

Anxiety problems will cause you to worry all the time about your thoughts. You will always be thinking into the future, imagining the worst, and trying to get prepared. Being anxious gives a great deal of energy to your brain because it is a survival mechanism. If we didn't have anxiety, we wouldn't survive. Given the mental and physical energy that anxiety creates, however, it is very hard to get thoughts out of your head.

If you have mood swings, you may find that one day you have no problem whatsoever taking thoughts captive, but then the next day it is all you can do to think a positive thought of any kind. One day you have lots of energy, the next you have none. The cycle of all of this may cause you to give up all together.

If your brain is rather obsessive, you will have repetitive thoughts and you will think that you simply can't get them out of your mind. We all do it to some extent. For example, I am writing this during Christmas and at least once a day, the words to some Christmas song come into my brain and I sing that song about fifty times before I move on to the next one. The problem, of course, is that if the thought you are thinking about repetitively is a negative or sinful one, you are not doing a very good job taking thoughts captive.

I have listed just the basic brain health problems that can really stymie us in taking thoughts captive. There are many others. It may be important for you to consult with a professional about a diagnosis before you decide that you have a problem. Many of us are guilty of self-diagnosis, which can be very dangerous. Only a medical doctor or licensed psychologist, therapist, social worker, or pastoral counselor is capable of making accurate diagnoses. In addition to the possibility of looking at the brain, which only a medical doctor can do, there are a variety of psychological tests that can be helpful to professionals in assessment.

Every one of the diagnoses I have described, even though they are very much related to conditions in the brain, can also have spiritual components. There is nothing quite like a deep, personal relationship with God to improve the functioning of the brain. I personally believe that surrendering our lives can have a tremendous effect on anxiety and depression, for example. I have also seen that many people who have tried to make such a surrender, and even think that they have, are frustrated when it doesn't always magically transform their overall mental health. The Bible describes some individuals who both had a relationship with God and suffered from mental health issues. If you read the Psalms, for example, you can feel the change in David's soul from a state of depression and anxiety to deep faith and serenity.

Knowing all of this suggests to me that it is often very important to consult with a mental health professional *and* a pastor. Pastors, particularly those who have training in counseling and/or spiritual direction, can make an assessment of a person's spiritual condition. The brain and the spirit are so intertwined that one can't be treated without the other. It really should be a combination of psychological, medical, and spiritual intervention that restores the brain to full functioning and health.

⊛ KEY POINT

It is very important that you get an accurate assessment of the functioning of your brain. Never rely on yourself to make that diagnosis. Restoring your brain to its optimal health is vital to taking every thought captive.

⊛ KEY QUESTIONS

- Have you ever been diagnosed with a mental health disorder?

- If so, what did you do about it?

- Have others around you suggested that you get help for mental health issues?

- Have problems with mood, anxiety, or attention ever affected your school, work, or relationships?

Self-Medication of the Brain

Many of us don't like talking about mental health or brain issues. We don't think of it as particularly Christian or mature, and we don't like admitting those kinds of problems. I think we are getting better at it, but if we don't feel comfortable talking about it, what do we do?

I believe that many of us have learned to cope on our own. It is in fact the ways we learn to cope that often lead to the very thoughts we are trying to avoid. Let's start with an easy one. Are there any of you who can't get started in the morning without that first cup of coffee? The fact is that coffee does stimulate blood flow to the brain by increasing heart rate and blood pressure and does definitely have a very short-term mood-elevating effect on the brain.

I really don't want to take away your caffeine. Most of you probably use it in moderation. I'm hooked on Diet Coke. In fact, I'm drinking one now as I write and I'm hoping it is helping to stimulate my creativity. There are times, however, when my cardiologist tells me to cut back.

What about nicotine? It is a stimulant and has a mood-elevating quality, even though we associate smoking with relaxing or calming down. Alcohol also has the same effect, improving our mood for a short time. This is why some use it to escape difficult feelings and life situations. Then there are all of the other drugs available to us that can either elevate or depress our mood.

All of the various chemicals we can ingest act on various centers in the brain. Even the food we eat can be broken down into various chemical substances in our body that have mood-elevating or depressing effects on the brain. Some of us are born with greater vulnerabilities in those areas of the brain and may be more likely to develop a dependency or addiction to a substance or substances. Stressful life events can trigger a greater need in some to eat, smoke, drink, or use various chemicals to relieve that stress. Everything we do has effects on the brain. An average day for many of us is an ongoing attempt to mood-manage our brains.

If you are addicted to a substance (including food), you have probably experienced craving. This kind of craving is different from the once-in-a-great-while craving you might have for chocolate or your favorite pie or drink. Addictive craving is like a five-alarm fire in the brain. Because the brain has grown so accustomed to the substance, whatever it may be, it demands to have more of it. When thoughts of the substances take over, the brain and all thoughts become rather irrational and you have become physiologically dependent.

Here is a disclaimer: if you are struggling with addiction to substances, your brain is having physiologically demanding thoughts. If you think that reading this or any book can help you get rid of those thoughts, you would be mistaken. Put this book down and get help. Addiction treatment can be very effective if you are willing to stop. Your issues with thoughts are unmanageable and will demand professional intervention.

For most of you reading this book, taking an inventory of what you do every day to raise or lower your mood through the use of various substances might be enough to get you to stop the use of those that you think can have negative long-term effects. If any addicts are still reading, please know that this book will be helpful in your effort to avoid relapse, but only after you have achieved a long period of initial sobriety or abstinence from the substance.

There are other ways to self-medicate in addition to the substances that we ingest. Brain research over the last twenty years has allowed us to see (remember brain radiology) that various behaviors, even thoughts of the behavior, can cause your body to produce chemicals. Some of these chemicals can also have mood-elevating or mood-depressing effects on the brain.

Any behavior that is new, exciting, or dangerous can produce the hormone adrenaline. Gambling is risky, for example, and the high of that danger is due to adrenaline. Likewise, working at challenging tasks, particularly under deadlines, can raise adrenaline. Shopping and the hunt for that special bargain are exciting. Driving fast, climbing mountains, or bungee jumping produces a rush. When addictionologists claim that gambling, work, shopping, or other challenging activities can be addictive, they are referring to the high adrenaline these behaviors create, which has a natural antidepressant quality. The key to this kind of addiction is that you don't need to go to a store or work through some pusher on the street to get the supply of the drug, because it's naturally produced. In some cases, even just thinking about the activity, or fantasizing, can be exciting enough to produce the chemicals.

There are other activities that can have sedative or mood-depressing qualities. Reading is one, as is watching mindless TV. Watching sporting events may produce adrenaline, but otherwise TV or reading has a rather hypnotic effect. There are people, of course, who might claim to be addicted to reading or watching TV. This is not due to particular brain chemicals that are produced, but rather to the trance-like state. As such, it is not very different from meditation. At times, in moderation, these activities can be relaxing and stress-reducing and, again, if done in moderation, can be good for the body. It is when a person relies on them for hours every day that they become a problem.

Since I normally work in the field of sex addiction, I have been very interested in what brain chemicals cause sex to be addictive. There are a number of brain chemicals at work in sexual addiction because of the sexual response cycle in the brain. This is somewhat complicated and I will try to simplify it. The key is that even simply thinking about sex can cause a physical reaction in the body. The main center of the brain that is involved in controlling sexual activity, in layman's terms, is the pleasure center. It is located deep inside the brain and is involved in everything that gives us pleasure. The pleasure center reminds us that certain substances and activities produce pleasure.

Perhaps you need to remember that pleasure can simply be felt when we eat. The memory center part of the brain then reminds us to eat because it is pleasurable. Likewise, sex is pleasurable and we are reminded to do it again because it is vital to the reproduction of humankind. Both eating and sex are important survival activities, and the pleasure center part of our brains is inherently involved in controlling that.

On the front end of the sexual response cycle is arousal or excitement. If the sex we're thinking about is exciting, which it almost always is, then adrenaline gets the body ready for sex. Breathing gets faster and the heart pumps faster, giving parts of the body increased blood flow. In the brain the adrenaline has an upper effect.

The main drug involved in arousal or sexual pleasure is dopamine. This is the ultimate feel-good brain chemical. Other substances and some activities elevate dopamine, which is the favorite drug of many who don't even know its name. They are really dopamine junkies. Remember that even sexual fantasies can release this drug in the pleasure center of the brain. It is quite the high.

Sex involves touch. We either engage in touch with our spouse, or in the case of some singles, and yes, some married people, sometimes ourselves in an act of masturbation. This releases another powerful sex drug—oxytocin. Nursing mothers are very familiar with this because it is the chemical that bonds a child to the mother during nursing. This drug gives us a feeling of well-being and connection. If children don't get touched enough, not enough oxytocin is produced and they might experience what is called failure to thrive. These children will stop growing and, in extreme cases, will even die. When we grow older, we still need human touch and, therefore, oxytocin. This drug is also a natural upper.

When sexual activity produces an orgasm, a whole other set of brain chemicals are produced in the pleasure center—the catecholamines. These drugs have been compared to heroin and produce the euphoria that is experienced right after sex. There is also a calming experience with these drugs that causes a person to "come down" from the pleasure cycle in a very pleasing way. The whole cycle takes us up, helps us feel connected, and then euphorically brings us back down. The memory center of the brain remembers all of this and wants to do it again and again.

What we in the addiction field know is that some people have the vulnerability to become chemically tolerant to all of these drugs. The brain will then demand more and more to achieve the same effect. This is why sex can become an addiction just like a drug addict experiences. A sex addict will need to engage in more and more sex or more exciting and dangerous sex over time to achieve the same cycle of mood elevation, connection, and euphoria.

Through looking at the brain with FMRI radiology, doctors discovered that showing a group of women a picture of the man they loved had the power to produce the catecholamines. This brain chemistry and the associated tolerance and craving has led many to say that not only is there a sex addiction, but there is also the possibility of a romance or love addiction.

The important part of all of this to remember is that we often seek to medicate our feelings of loneliness, boredom, stress, anger, or depression with the powerful brain chemicals available to us through sex and romance. Do you see the possibilities for self-medicating anxiety, depression, mood swings, and ADD through the use of a variety of substances we ingest or behaviors that produce natural mood-altering chemicals?

Please know that the thoughts you are trying to take captive may be related to these powerful substances. We can obsess about them and be driven by them. Our whole reality can center on them. If we are going to win our battle to take these thoughts captive, we must be prepared to give up certain substances or behaviors that drive them.

● KEY POINT

Our thoughts often get preoccupied with substances and behaviors that we are using to self-medicate various problems in our brain.

✸ KEY QUESTIONS

- Have you ever felt that you were dependent or addicted to a substance or behavior?

- If so, what have you done about it?

- On a daily basis, what substances do you ingest to alter your mood?

- Likewise, what behaviors do you do every day that either raise or lower your mood?

Self-medicating can lead us down very destructive paths, including addiction. There are healthy alternatives to fixing the brain. The following are a variety of strategies that can be used to improve brain health.

Pharmacology

During the course of my life, I have seen the dramatic increase in the development of various drugs that can be used to treat mental health and brain disorders. Are some of you old enough to remember the days when people with severe mental conditions were sent to a hospital just to keep them away from the public? Very little if any actual treatment took place there, and these unfortunate people were sometimes never seen in public again. One of the first of these kinds of hospitals was called Bethlehem Hospital in London. It was such a crazy place that it led to the use of the word "bedlam," which is "Bethlehem" said with a Cockney accent. There are many stereotypical images of these hospitals, such as in the movie *One Flew over the Cuckoo's Nest.* Needless to say, there have been some interesting approaches to mental health over the years.

Are you aware that these hospitals were literally cleaned out of patients with the advent of new drugs to treat these severe mental health issues? Today, most hospitals have mental health units, but they are there to treat issues such as severe depression in a short period of time. Usually, a person is there just long enough to get diagnosed and then put on the right and hopefully effective drug(s).

It seems to me that the variety of drugs that are available today to treat depression, anxiety, mood disorders, obsessive-compulsive disorder, and attention deficit hyperactivity disorder (ADHD) increases all the time. One really needs to be a medical doctor in order to stay up with how often the field changes, which means there are more and more answers to help people who suffer with various conditions.

Very occasionally I run across a person who objects to taking drugs. Some just don't like the idea of them period, while others believe that it is a matter of faith and that taking drugs is somehow unchristian. I once talked to a man who was drinking too much, smoking, using marijuana, overeating, and looking at pornography all the time. He told me, "Taking medication is just not good for you." I told him, "If I get what you're saying, ingesting or smoking various substances is okay, as long as it is not medically prescribed."

There is no doubt that you have to be careful, get the correct diagnosis, and take the right drugs in the right doses. There still might be side effects, but imagine what the effects might be if you don't take the drug and your mental health issues get out of control. I am certainly not saying that taking medication will automatically help you take every thought captive, but without them, some people can't even face getting up in the morning.

Certainly those struggling with addiction and ADD will notice a day-and-night difference if they get proper treatment and medication. I have known men who couldn't get sober for years, and then, finally, they got treated for ADD and found that getting sober was at last possible. Remember, I'm only talking about returning the brain to some state of normalcy to give it a fair chance to make the right thought choices. No addict I know, including myself, would suggest that addiction could be cured by taking a medication.

I have always thought of medications as the tools science occasionally gives us to be healthy and able to fulfill God's plan for our lives. Without the drug insulin I would have died in 1976. I still take it today, and it has kept me relatively normal and healthy. It doesn't cure me of diabetes, but by taking it I have been able to be a husband, father, and pastoral counselor. On insulin, I have traveled the world and look forward to doing so for a long time. On insulin, I learned how to take my sexual thoughts captive and how to become sexually pure.

Therapy and Counseling

Since this is what I do most days, either with individuals or with groups, I am rather invested in it. Counseling and therapy can be vital elements in a person's healing journey and, therefore, in his or her ability to take every thought captive.

There are a vast array of professionals who perform therapy and counseling, and there are also many types of therapy and counseling. There are professionals who specialize in various kinds of mental health disorders. Likewise, there are therapies that work best with different individual and relationship issues. There is individual counseling, marriage counseling, family counseling, and group counseling. There are counseling centers that provide outpatient help. This means you will probably go to counseling once a week for an hour or two. There is intense counseling where you might go to a certain center that specializes in the problem you are having, and the process involves you being there for one to two weeks and many hours each day. There are inpatient programs where you go and are hospitalized for a month or more. These programs are typically for some sort of addiction but may also treat other individual and relational issues. Finally, there are workshops and seminars that teach about various problems and may include a therapy component.

It is easy to get confused by what's available. You may need counseling about what type of counseling you need! The Internet is a great source of information about all of this. You can google any type of problem and find a clear definition of it and what kinds of counseling or therapy have been shown to be most effective. The Internet can point you to Web sites about the problem you are having. Some of these are clearinghouses that may have lists of professionals who specialize in treating it. There are certain organizations that seek to train and even certify counselors and therapists to do what they do. For Christians, the largest of these, for example, is the American Association of Christian Counselors (AACC).[5] Members of the AACC can be lay counselors, therapists, social workers, pastors, or psychologists. The key to a group like this is that all members must demonstrate their clinical competence and also sign a statement of faith attesting to their Christian beliefs.

I believe it is impossible to perform therapy or counseling without a faith in him who created and sustains us. I would not be well today if it were not for my faith in God's only Son, Jesus Christ. My faith has been the foundation of my recovery from sexual sin, anxiety, and depression. The faith that my wife and I share has been the foundation of the success of our marriage today. Along the way, we have both been blessed individually and as a couple with caring and skilled counselors.

The main focus of any counseling or therapy is how it will help you with your thoughts; thoughts about yourself, others, your calling, and about God. Most of us develop thoughts about all of this beginning as children. Our thoughts are shaped by how we are raised and develop over time. Others—like your parents, siblings, teachers, and friends—model behaviors that become attitudes, values, and beliefs; in short, thoughts about everything there is. All of your experiences in life shape your thoughts. If you were somehow abused emotionally, physically, or sexually, those experiences shape how you think about yourself and others.

I am the survivor of sexual abuse. My thoughts about relationships and sex were profoundly affected by that experience. Those thoughts were shameful, lustful, and totally misguided. They were what I call today, "The lies I believed." These lies would invade my mind at the worst of times. To take them captive I had to first learn all about them and then understand that God's truth was so very different from these lies. A skillful counselor helped me to see, for example, that I didn't cause the abuse and that God, my Father, loved me the whole time and wept with me for what happened.

Some of you didn't have your basic needs met when you were growing up. Not being loved, paid attention to, heard and understood, blessed for who you are and not what you do, or helped to feel safe in the world, can be just as damaging to the way you think as being invaded. If you never got what you needed, your thoughts might be that you are not lovable, good enough, or worth anything. You may have developed lies about what false substitutes will satisfy those needs. I used to think that the women who smiled at me from the pages of pornography would satisfy my need for female nurturing. I also used to think that if I just worked hard enough and accomplished enough important work, then I would get the true blessing I so longed for.

Some of the thoughts you need to take captive are the ones that simply seem to intrude or show up without warning. I have a client who was physically abused as a child. Often frightening thoughts about his own safety just break in. There are sounds, tones of voice, and sights such as a belt that can send him into anxious and panicky thoughts. You see, the physical abuse helped to develop the survival parts of his brain to quickly react so as to protect himself. Today, that developed brain is so finely tuned that it will react to the slightest stimulus that reminds him of the abuse.

There is plenty of good news about all of this. The value of therapy and counseling is that all of the messages, lies, modeling, and intrusive thoughts can be healed and corrected in the truth of God's love for us. It will usually take time and skilled professionals to help with this, but I would not do what I do if I hadn't seen great miracles of healing happen.

Earlier in this chapter I wrote about brain scans and one of the pioneers in doing this, Dr. Daniel Amen. In 2002 I went out to see him for the first time and he offered to scan my brain. When I saw one of the pictures of it, Dr. Amen explained to me that I had a pattern in my brain that has been identified in those people who have experienced some form of trauma. At this point Dr. Amen knew nothing about my history, and I was amazed when, just by looking at my brain, he said, "You must be a sexual abuse survivor." When I explained to him what happened to me, he went on to say, "You must have had a lot of therapy because if you hadn't, given what you've told me, your brain would be a lot worse."

Thanks be to God that help exists and that the brain has the ability to heal even from the worst forms of trauma.

Nutrition and Supplements

As anybody who knows me will tell you, I am no expert in nutrition or any form of healthy supplements. I can read, however, and over the years I have noticed the growing number of studies that confirm how a healthy diet can be wonderful for your brain. Any of the conditions that I have been describing can definitely be helped by healthy eating and supplements. One example is Omega 3, which can be found in fish oil and can also be obtained by taking Omega 3 capsules. It has tremendously powerful healing effects on the brain. One of my favorite foods that are rich in antioxidants, blueberries, is likewise very good for the brain. I encourage you to read for yourself and decide what foods and supplements are right for you. Each of Dr. Amen's books, such as *Change Your Brain, Change Your Life;* or *Change Your Brain, Change Your Body;* and finally, *Making a Good Brain Great,* have very specific recommendations about diet and nutrition for very specific parts of the brain.

Over the years I have found that when I ask any one of the array of doctors I see as a diabetic about nutrition, they all say pretty much the same thing, "That's a great idea." That's all they say. As I've realized, they have almost no training in their medical education about nutrition. So, with this one, I recommend that if you need help, ask to be referred to a dietician or find someone else who is trained in this. Most of us have read or seen lots of information about how to eat for our hearts and other parts of our bodies, but really no information about how to eat for our brain, the most important organ in our bodies because it controls all the other parts. This is truly a quest where we are on our own.

Exercise

These days it is very easy to do research on any topic on the Internet. I remember being in graduate school in the seventies and needing to go into a library, deal with the smell of must, and then track down obscure journals from rows and stacks of them. Then you had to copy them at five cents a page. Still to this day, I have boxes and boxes of articles that my wife routinely asks me about getting rid of. When she does, I think about all of those nickels.

Today, however, while writing this book, I went to the Internet and in the space of two minutes found over one hundred articles about the benefits of exercise on the brain.[6] To summarize, regular exercise has been proven to help

- Reduce stress
- Ward off feelings of anxiety and depression
- Boost self-esteem
- Improve sleep

Research further suggests that the reason for these benefits is because exercise

- Releases brain chemicals and endorphins that produce a feeling of well-being
- Reduces immune system chemicals that can worsen depression
- Raises body temperature, which can have a calming effect

Research does not suggest that there is any particular kind of exercise better than others. The key is that whatever it is, it must raise the heart rate for at least twenty minutes. Perhaps one of the thoughts you are trying to take captive is the one that tells you that you don't have time to exercise. The truth is that if you want to improve your brain and its ability to control your thoughts, you will need to do something. Obviously, all of this exercise will have many other benefits for your general health.

Social Support

When I was in graduate school, I was fascinated with how stress affects the entire body. What I learned was so astounding to me. Stress can contribute to every ailment known to humanity. Most interesting was the conclusion that stress has a profound effect on the immune system. If stress impairs the immune system enough, things even as major as cancer cells will not be stopped. As in the previous section on exercise, there are literally hundreds of articles that can be found on the Internet that demonstrate this point and are based on sound, empirical research.

Controlling stress is vital to the health of all parts of the body, including the brain. Back in graduate school I was deeply interested in what would help get rid of stress. I have already talked about many of the things we can do. Meditation is very powerful. Diet and nutrition play a role. Exercise is very helpful. The king of all strategies, however, is the ability to give up control, to stop trying to micromanage all aspects of life. Researchers have consistently shown that people who have a

spiritual foundation to their lives, in which they are able to surrender control of their lives to God, have almost no stress.

The people who are more likely to be able to do this are
those people who have strong social support. Hundreds of
health studies have shown that people who have a strong community around them will get sick much less often than loners
do. In short, we all need to belong and be included. It is often
the encouragement, love, help, nurturing, and prayers of others
that prevent us from having stress and all of its consequences.

To take every thought captive, you will need a strong and
healthy brain that is free of stress. Stress does a profound number on the brain. Having support around you will go a long
way toward having a healthy brain. In *The 7 Principles of Highly Accountable Men*, I wrote that belonging to various kinds
of support groups is an essential part of being accountable.
Belonging to groups provides you with an army of support for
whatever you are trying to stop or start. Do you now see that
if you are able to participate in such groups, it has enormously
positive effects on your entire body, particularly your brain
because of all the stress-relieving qualities of groups?

Social support can come from families, groups of friends,
coworkers, and (last but not least) church. In fact, the church
connection has been shown by researchers to greatly improve
health. In a 2006 study by researchers from the Human Population Laboratories of the Public Health Institute and the California
Department of Health Services, and the University of California,
Berkeley, found that people who attended religious services
once a week had significantly lower risks of death compared to

those who attended less frequently or never, even after adjusting for age, health behaviors, and other risk factors.[7]

So, evidently, going to church will have universal health benefits. I believe this is because it provides social support, relieves stress, and improves brain health.

● KEY POINT

Healthy brains take every thought captive. Unhealthy brains don't heal.

● KEY QUESTIONS

- Have you ever gone to therapy and was it a good experience?

- If so, or if not, would you be willing to try it again?

- Do you have people you trust to advise you about who to see for therapy or counseling?

- How is your diet and do you take supplements?

- What is your exercise pattern like?

- What groups do you regularly participate in?

Transforming the Brain Is a Physical Reality

What we have been talking about in this chapter is that the brain can be healthy—it can heal and can literally be rewired in such a way that you will be able to take every thought captive. I have seen this personally. A number of years ago I participated in a study that was taking place at the Psychiatry Department of Vanderbilt University. The purpose of the study was to observe the electrical patterns of the brain in reaction to various visual stimuli, mainly pornography. FMRI radiological brain scanning was used during the study. Participants were shown various video clips, including a ninety-second clip of a pornographic video, and the changes in the electrical activity of the brain were observed. Other parts of the body were also being monitored to check for sexual arousal.

All of this is very technical. To put it simply, it was shown that the connections in the brain from the visual center to the pleasure center where sexual activity is produced form a pleasure pathway. When the pleasure center is thus activated, that part of the brain "lights up." Corresponding changes in the body indicated that sexual arousal was being experienced. I was asked to be a research subject because, at that time, I had over fifteen years of sexual sobriety. I had not acted in sexually sinful ways and had learned very well how to take my sexual thoughts captive. When I was scanned and saw the pornographic video, I didn't experience any feelings of sexual arousal.

I came out of the FMRI scanner and felt pretty good about myself. I was so "healthy" that not even looking at pornography had the same effect as it once would have. The researchers confirmed that based on their monitoring, I had not been sexually aroused, so, naturally, I thought my pleasure pathway and pleasure center had not lit up. That turned out to not be true. The scan revealed that both of these were "lit up like a Christmas tree." I asked the chief researcher, Dr. Peter Martin, how this could be. I knew that once the pleasure center is activated, it automatically sends signals down to the rest of the body to get ready for sex, and yet I had no such reaction.

Dr. Martin told me (these results have never been officially published) that what they observed in my brain was what he called an override. This computer term means that my brain literally had new neurological pathways that overrode the original pathways. I had previously looked at pornography for twenty-five years, and Dr. Martin said that all of that memory was stored in my brain. When I saw pornography for the first time in over fifteen years, all of that memory got "lit up." He then said that because of all of my training, discipline, and ability to take every thought captive, my brain had created new pathways that prevented the sexual thoughts from creating sexual arousal. Pornography and all of its ill effects were still stored in my brain, but new pathways had prevented that part of my brain from producing unhealthy sexual behavior.

This confirmed to me that what we put in our brain over the course of a lifetime stays there. That is the consequence of sin. The good news, however, is that Paul was right: our brain can be transformed by the grace of God and made new again. Dr. Martin warned me that it was only through all of my discipline that this new effect took place. If I ever stopped this discipline, my brain could always revert back to the old patterns. His message to me was, "Keep doing what you're doing."

If you are interested, there is a very good and rather new book that explains the ability of the brain to wire itself for either sin or purity.[8] It is written by a good friend of mine, Dr. William Struthers, who is a brain scientist. The key is the conscious choices we make to lead a pure life. We can't expect that our brains will never be tempted or that our sinful memories will never again stimulate us. We can expect, however, that through healthy choices and discipline, we don't have to act out in sinful ways. We can learn to take every thought captive and doing so will literally transform the brain.

I have been saving the best for last in the final three chapters. Read on to see how to achieve brain transformation in the deepest spiritual ways.

4
TAKING FANTASIES CAPTIVE

In this chapter and the next I want to teach you the long-term strategies to taking thoughts captive. By that I mean, if you master the methods I will describe in chapters 4 and 5, you won't need the strategies in chapters 1–3 because there won't be any inappropriate thoughts to take captive. Don't get me wrong, you will still need those early strategies at first, and perhaps at other times in your life. These long-term strategies will require some patience and endurance.

In this chapter I want you to take a look at your fantasies with me. "Wait a minute," you say, "getting rid of fantasies is exactly why I got your book. Now you want me to look at them?!" I want you to begin to think about the core idea of this chapter. Fantasies are not the enemy to get rid of at all costs, to avoid, to be ashamed of, or to beat yourself up about. Fantasies are pictures, images, and stories that you have created in your mind. Now you say, "Wait another minute, I don't remember creating them." You probably don't consciously sit down one day and say, "Let's see, what fantasy will I create today?"

The truth is, however, that your mind did create them. It picked and chose from all of your past experiences, actual events you remember, and added images of events that you simply create. Basically you cut and paste until you have a video tape in your brain of what you'd love to see actually happen. It is your imagination; you are a film director and you are writing the ideal script of your future life.

What drives all of this creativity? The longing of your soul does. The legitimate longings of your soul for love, nurturing, kindness, understanding, attention, affirmation, blessing, safety, and belonging are seeking to be fulfilled. The challenge is that, based on your memory, your soul may not always know how to get those needs met in healthy ways. The ways of the world present lots of messages about how to get needs met. Our mind and our soul have been told how to get needs met by the culture around us. Advertising at its best tells us that we will be truly happy if we buy certain products.

Think about this: every fantasy I've ever had is really a message from the soul about what it deeply needs and desires.

Perhaps some examples from different categories of fantasies will help you see my point. Have you ever had a sport's fantasy? I have many, but let me tell you about just a few of them. As a boy I longed to be a famous tennis player. I practiced, took a few lessons, and joined my high school team. I envisioned eventually playing in the famous tennis tournaments of the world, winning them, and then (when I was famous) I would use the platform I had to witness for Christ. I even used that plan to pray to God to convince him of the need I had for him to turn me into a great tennis player.

God, however, had other plans. He already knew, for example, that he had not created me with great athletic talent. I was a fairly good player, and in my junior year of high school, I was playing in the Illinois State High School Tennis Tournament. I was doing very well, cruising along, winning handily, when in my next round my opponent came on the court. He was a very small, young looking "kid" who I thought was way too young to even be playing in the tournament. I said to myself, "I am going to have my way with this kid, go on to the next round, on to the state finals, and then on to tennis glory." Well, that was the plan. The "kid" turned out to be a young Jimmy Connors, who turned out to be one of the greatest players in the history of tennis. He had his way with me that day, and he is the one who went on to tennis glory. I can't say that he has ever witnessed for God, or anyone else for that matter. Needless to say, I was a little disappointed with God for not answering my prayers.

Now, do you ever think that I replay that match in my mind? Of course I do, and who do you think wins in my fantasy? Yes, forty-three years later when I think about that match, I figure out a way to win, and in my fantasy, I go on to tennis glory. You see, one of the desires of the soul that a fantasy can fulfill is the "correction" of a situation from the past. Fantasies can replay previous events, but this time there is a different result.

● KEY POINT

Fantasies can seek to fulfill a desire of the soul for a different result to a previous life event.

Think about your own fantasies. Have you ever "corrected" a previous athletic event? There are a lot of them for me. My senior year in high school the basketball team was expected to win the Illinois state tournament. We were ranked number one all year long. In the state quarterfinal game, called the Super Sectional, our team came up against a team on which Jim Brewer played. We didn't know it at the time, but he was destined for basketball glory and later played for the University of Minnesota and the Milwaukee Bucks. That night Jim Brewer had his way with us and we lost a heartbreaking game. Our dreams of a state championship were dashed.

Almost twenty years later, a movie called *Hoosiers* was released in which a small-town team wins the Indiana state championship over a team from a much larger school. One of the characters in that movie, Jimmy, sinks a shot at the buzzer to win the game. In my fantasy, who do you think gets to play Jimmy?

In the final scene, Jimmy is carried off the court by his adoring fans. How many times do you think I have watched that movie? I lost count but at least twenty times. This fantasy corrects a previous loss that caused my soul pain. It also fulfills a second type of soul desire because it brings me great glory and admiration. In my fantasy I am affirmed and praised and really get to be somebody. If my soul is longing for these things and has been all my life, even a movie fantasy can fulfill that longing.

● KEY POINT

If our soul longs for love, nurturing, acceptance, praise, safety, or inclusion, to name a few, a fantasy can create a future in which we receive all those things.

Do you ever have money fantasies? These make up a second category of fantasies. Most of us dream of having more money than we have. I was raised in a pastor's home, and while we had enough money, it never seemed to me that we had as much money as others did. When my father was successful, he was called to an affluent church in an affluent suburb of Chicago. I thought all the kids I went to high school with came from wealthy families, and that was, in fact, true. Any money fantasies I have today correct the fact that I wasn't wealthy back then, because in my imagination, I have lots of money.

A while ago one of our state lotteries reached an astounding $230 million. I normally don't believe in buying lottery tickets, but my fantasies got the better of me. I prayed to God, "Lord, you know I would do a lot of great things with that money. I tithe for one thing, and if you let me win, my church would get $23 million. Either tell me the six numbers or just allow me to be in the right place at the right time to buy the winning ticket." I'm sure I would have given lots of money away, but I would still have lots of it left. Then would come houses, cars, boats, and vacations. So first of all, this fantasy corrects my perceived poverty of youth. It would also bring me lots of admiration and acceptance. People love and respect those who have lots of money.

Think of all the poor people in the world who scrape together enough money to buy a lottery ticket or go to a casino hoping for the big win. Perhaps they are even homeless. Don't you think they have fantasies of winning money because their souls simply long for a safe place to sleep and food to eat? You can understand how money fantasies lead some to gambling problems, compulsive debt, or even theft.

A third category of fantasies centers on achievement. Have you ever dreamed of becoming the boss, getting a promotion, or receiving an advanced degree? Maybe you dream of being a big movie star and seeing yourself in the pages of *People* magazine. If you've ever fantasized about becoming a famous athlete who makes lots of money and is known by millions, you can see how athletic, money, and achievement fantasies are combined.

I have a friend who has never felt very good about himself with regard to success; it is a part of his larger sense of shame. I have watched over the years as he has tried one get-rich scheme after another. He has started businesses, dabbled in real estate, and traded commodities, yet he somehow never succeeds. My belief is that his soul longs for the relief of his shame and that he fantasizes that becoming a successful businessman will fulfill that desire. When he fantasizes about these things, his true calling as a teacher and counselor gets overlooked. When our fantasies conflict with God's call, I doubt they will ever come true. In the next chapter I will write more about the difference between fantasy and vision.

Fantasies, like my friend's, can have multiple purposes. His desire to be successful and his fantasy of himself as a rich businessman are attempts to achieve two desires. First, he seeks to correct the failures of his past that stretch all the way back to his childhood. Notice that what is often being corrected is a sense of loss. It might be, as in this case, the feeling that he never lived up to the expectations he had for himself or that others had for him. Not to have achieved those expectations is a loss, and the fantasy corrects it. Second, the fantasy seeks to fulfill the desire to be affirmed, admired, and accepted. While the fantasy is about making money, money is really secondary to the desire to be appreciated and loved.

I find that one of our biggest desires is the desire to be blessed. What it is really all about is the longing to be loved just for who we are and not what we do. Affirmation is the desire to be recognized for what we have done, while blessing is the desire for recognition of who we are as persons. The concept of blessing is very biblical. At the time of Jesus' baptism, God spoke to him and said, "This is my Son, whom I love; with him I am well pleased" (Matt. 3:17). Jesus hadn't really done any public ministry yet for which he could be affirmed, but God blessed him by saying he was pleased with him.

Did you get words of blessing like that from your earthly mother or father? Were they glad that you were born? Did they ever tell you they were proud of you? One of my clients told me he doesn't remember that his mother ever smiled when he entered the room. That is a powerful memory. It is not about what his mother did; it is about what she didn't do. This man felt deep down in his soul that she was never glad to see him and that she didn't really care.

Blessing is about that smile, a sense of interest and enthusiasm in who you are. Blessing is about being celebrated. One exercise I have most of the people I work with do is to ask themselves what happened on their birthday. Was there a party? Were there presents? Were positive stories told about them on those days?

Examine your heart carefully because blessing is really important. Those of you who don't feel as though you received it may experience shame or a sense of worthlessness. This is the feeling that you don't really matter or that you can never be enough or get things right.

Before we go any further, I would like to emphasize that to understand this you don't have to get to some angry place where you start thinking, "My parents did an awful job!" My experience over the years has taught me that parents mostly do the best they possibly can. Many of them, however, are in pain of some kind and don't really know how to love as they should. All parents make mistakes; I know I have. In order to understand the feelings you may have inside, allow yourself to simply say that the journey of healing is about understanding the messages you carry inside. Some of them, based on how you were raised, may not be consistent with God's opinion of you. God is the only parent who can truly love us as we ought to be loved, and he is certainly the only one who can truly bless us.

Parents aren't the only ones who contribute to our feeling of being blessed. The kids in the neighborhood or at school, teachers, coaches, leaders, and pastors are all people who either help us feel accepted, included, admired, appreciated, and affirmed or the complete opposite. I always thought, for example, that my fourth grade teacher had an angry scowl on her face when I was in the room. Today I know that she was a lonely, single, and frustrated older woman. Her scowl was about who she was and what she experienced in life. When I was nine years old, however, I thought I was dirt in her classroom. There didn't seem to be anything I could do right. I remember thinking when I graduated from my doctoral program, "I wish I could walk into Miss Loyd's classroom now and show her my diploma. She would either be shocked, or she would finally smile."

Remember fantasies and what they can tell us about the longing of our soul? Do you see that if you never felt blessed, accepted, included, or affirmed, your fantasies of success, fame, or achievement may be your attempt to solve this feeling?

Judy,[9] for example, grew up in New York City. Her father, a physician, was never home. This was mostly a good thing because when he was home, he was always critical. Judy's father criticized her grades, her friends, her achievements, and everything she ever did. Judy's mother was also the recipient of this criticism and became so depressed she had to occasionally be hospitalized. This left Judy at home to try and please her dad, which she never did.

When I met Judy, she had earned a college degree, three master's degrees, a PhD, and had just graduated from law school. She had married a very passive man who minded his own business and never seemed to get upset about anything. Do you see what Judy has done? She has married the opposite of her father. Her husband was safe. Through various academic degrees, she has been trying to find approval or blessing. She is constantly lonely, depressed, and shameful, despite the fact that everyone around her is tremendously impressed with her accomplishments.

Judy, now a practicing lawyer, came to counseling because she was critical of her husband. She felt that he never did anything. He was, in fact, a nuclear physicist with a PhD who worked at an atomic reactor. But what Judy meant was that she felt he never did anything for her. She began to fantasize about other men. Thoughts would enter her brain about dashing, charismatic, and successful men. They smiled in her fantasies and always seemed glad to see her. They praised her and did wonderful things for her.

Judy fantasized about this mythical man long enough that she finally met one who fit the picture in her brain. He was another lawyer and paid her a lot of attention. He did smile whenever she entered the room. Do you know where this is going? Yes, she wound up having first an emotional affair with him, which eventually led to sex. Now her marriage is in shambles because her "passive" husband has asked for a divorce.

You be the therapist. What did Judy's fantasy really try to do? Her soul was longing for blessing and affirmation. There was still the longing of a little girl to be loved by a father. I should also say that Judy had accepted Christ, but had come to faith in a very black-and-white church that offered formulaic ways to please God. Judy consequently never felt that she pleased God either. So a dynamic and exciting man came along and seemed to be the living expression of the fantasies she had been having for years. Judy's fantasies were a message from her soul.

This story has introduced us to a fourth category of fantasies. So far we have talked about sports, money, and achievement. Judy had many fantasies about money and achievement, but what really brought her crashing down were fantasies about romance and sex. I believe that this category is the most pervasive in our modern culture. Everywhere you look there are sexual and romantic images being portrayed. Do an inventory in your own mind of how many you have encountered today. Include TV, magazines, advertising, music, and movies in your list. When you're at the grocery store, ask yourself several questions: If the store you're in sells books, what is the largest category of books? If the store sells magazines, what are the titles of the articles about? When you're checking out, what images are being projected by the magazines displayed in the check-out lane? If your grocery store is like the ones I go to, the answers would be romance novels, sexual topics, and scantily clad women.

The truth is that our culture is infatuated with sex and romance and, unfortunately, has so intertwined the two that we all know that the phrase "making love" is really about sex. How many movies have you seen where sex takes place either implicitly or explicitly between two people who are not married? The explosion of sex and dating sites on the Internet is beyond description. If I gave you statistics about this today as I write, by the time this book is published they would have grown.

All of this feeds our brains and excites us to fantasize about sex and romance. So let's go back to our first two principles of what fantasies can do and see how they apply. First, fantasies can replay past events with a different result. How many of you have ever said, "If I had just continued my relationship with my former girlfriend or boyfriend . . . ?" You may think, "No, I've never done that," but have you ever gone to a reunion hoping to see someone and how he or she looks today? Is the person married? Is he or she happy? Have you ever gone on one of the social networking sites to see if you could find someone from your past? Today there is an explosion of affairs that take place between people who first met in school and then years later have rediscovered each other.

Have you ever fantasized about the "one that got away"? Have you ever gone back to a previous relationship and turned it into a sexual fantasy? Were you ever rejected by someone and imagined a different outcome?

Now here's a really tough set of questions for those of you who are married. Whatever the state of your marriage, have you ever fantasized about your spouse saying or doing different things? In your fantasies is he or she kinder, gentler, more affirming, or does he or she passionately want to be with you? In your fantasies does the old flame still burn? Does your spouse say or do things that he or she has never done before? You might be trying to correct something from the past with your spouse. I have known men, for example, who re-create their honeymoon night, only in their fantasies it is more exciting and passionate, and sexual activities happen that have never happened.

The second principle that we looked at is that fantasies take us to a place where we receive the blessing, love, nurturing, and affirmation that we so desperately desire. In a sexual fantasy it is relatively easy to understand that the person who is the object of the fantasy has all of the affirming, caring, loving, nurturing, and pleasing characteristics the fantasizer desires. The object of the fantasy may be a person from the past, like the old high school boyfriend, who seemed to have those qualities so long ago. The person in the fantasy may be a movie or TV star or even a composite person constructed from people you actually know.

Certain sexual acts that are fantasized about can also be an attempt to get desires met. The most basic of these kinds of fantasies is the fantasy of someone who never says no to an invitation for sex. That person is always willing. As many of the men I work with tell me, "In my fantasies the women always really want me. They like me. They want to be with me. They are willing to do anything I want them to do." Can you see that if those men are not experiencing this kind of passion with their wives, they will make someone up in their minds who will be passionate?

Let's take what one of my mentors, Pat Carnes, calls a "gentleness break." Some of you may be feeling a sense of guilt or shame, particularly if I'm triggering some awareness of sinful fantasies. Remember that we are on a quest to understand the longings of our soul. Believe me, I will teach you later about how to fulfill those longings in healthy ways. For now, go easy on yourself and realize that your fantasies are your attempt to get what your heart desires; they do not mean you are a bad or awful person. They may mean you are a lonely, tired, sad, anxious, or deeply wounded person. Don't you think that God cares deeply about you and that he so much wants you to not be lonely or any of these other things? Stay with me. It's going to get a little worse, and then it will get a whole lot better.

When I was eleven years old I saw my first pornographic magazine. A friend of mine showed me one he had stolen from the local drug store. I will never forget opening up that first centerfold. It was the first time I had seen a naked woman, and my adolescent hormones were running wild. It was an electric feeling that was physically and emotionally powerful. The woman in the picture was smiling and seemed to be looking right at me, as if she wanted me to look at her. She seemed to be enjoying the fact that she was being looked at. My eleven-year-old self took it as an answer to the loneliness in my soul. Most eleven-year-old boys wonder if a girl will ever like them, just like girls wonder if boys will ever like them. My mother was not particularly good at emotional connection, and I don't remember her smiling a lot, if at all. But this woman did smile and did seem to want me. The combination of the physical sensation and the emotional perception was one that would drive me to look at pornography for the next twenty-three years.

Any time I felt lonely, left out, or that girls didn't like me, I just had to remember that picture or look at other pictures just like it. I never thought about that fantasy being something sinful. I liked it, it made me feel good, and I wasn't about to take it captive. I thought it was fulfilling my very real need. My education in sexuality therefore continued with pornography as my teacher. I learned that women always enjoy sex, or at least seem to, they never say no, and they will perform sexual acts without ever seeming disgusted by them. No one else around me at home, school, or church was talking about sex and correcting these misperceptions. In short, Hugh Hefner was the wise, older man who led the way.

My brain was on fire. Countless fantasies had come and gone through my mind. By the time I got married, Debbie didn't stand a chance. My expectations were so warped that there was no way she or any woman could ever really satisfy me. I continued to search in pornography and other sexual activities for that satisfaction and in doing so greatly defiled our relationship.

When I finally woke up, I began to wonder how to take all these thoughts captive. Gradually, through the help of wise counselors, I began to see the connection from my addiction to my youth, loneliness, and desires. It was only with that understanding that I began to look for healthy solutions. It was also only then that my sexual relationship with Debbie became what God really intended for it to be, a one-flesh union.

As a counselor I have heard over three thousand stories of how men fantasize and what they fantasize about. No matter how perverted or "bad" you consider it, if you tell me what you fantasize about, I will tell you what your soul desires. I've heard thoughts of sexual acts of the strangest types: sex with all kinds of other people, men and women; sex with animals; sex with various objects; sex in public places; sex with multiple partners at the same time; sex that involves giving and receiving pain; sex that involves exchanging your spouse for someone else's. I have heard stories of men who have had thousands of sexual partners, masturbated up to ten times a day, spend hundreds of thousands of dollars on prostitution, exhibited themselves, or spied on others.

Nevertheless, I haven't heard a story in which the person is not in a lot of pain and who is not trying to get some deep soul desires met. I can interpret these fantasies by simply calming my spirit and listening to what a person is saying. Even the most bizarre of sexual behaviors have either a positive association with an individual's childhood or some symbolic meaning. The most common example I run across is men who wish their wives would engage in oral sex with them. Receiving oral sex is highly symbolic of being totally "taken in" and thereby accepted. Yes, it is sexually stimulating and physically feels good, but do not discount the tremendously powerful emotional desire it represents. I challenge you to take your sexual thoughts captive and begin to ask yourself what they mean about the longing of your soul. Later I will suggest a questionnaire you can use to take your thoughts captive and interrogate them.

There is one more possibility for what fantasies can mean. They can replay past events that resulted in joy, excitement, accomplishment, or relief from some emotional pain. We can go back to our four basic categories, athletics, money, achievement, and sex/romance, to illustrate this possibility.

Have you ever followed the career of a professional athlete after that person retires? It takes a very special grace to make that transition. He or she has received so much acclaim, heard so much applause, and experienced a performance adrenaline high that is hard to come down from. If you have ever had similar experiences, do you ever relive those times? The other day I had a conversation with man who was recounting the story of the one home run he hit in little league. What became apparent to me was that this had been a temporary relief to a lonely twelve-year-old boy. Today he replays that event at times when he is feeling lonely or socially uncomfortable. Do you get the idea?

The same can be true for money. Have you ever relived a time when you received a special gift or won a special prize? Maybe you went through a period of relative prosperity and you go back to the glory days. It is actually this dynamic that drives compulsive gambling. Most gamblers know the odds of actually winning, but there was that one time when they "hit it big." The adrenaline reward of that was so powerful that they go back and try to duplicate it.

Some workaholics are trying to re-create the big success or score. I was talking to a salesman who had once received a big bonus for being salesman of the year. Every year he now fantasizes about doing that again. He came to me because his work hours were creating havoc for his family.

This last illustration transitions us to the achievement fantasies. Over the years I have worked with various celebrities from movie stars and rock stars to professional athletes. One of my rock star clients came to me because of repeated infidelities and several broken marriages. If you've ever been to a rock concert and seen women throw themselves at the band, you know how hard it would be to resist those temptations. So he asked me, "Doc, how do I get sober?" I said, "Maybe you need to stop performing." Understand that at this point he was already one of the most successful and wealthy rock stars of all time. He said to me, "I don't know if I could live without the rush of performance. Do you know how much money we make on every concert?"

The truth is that this star was addicted to the adrenaline rush of performing and the success that came with it. Interestingly enough, he was a recovering alcoholic and drug addict and had been sober for over ten years in AA. There is no twelve-step group for adrenaline, however. A person like this will really need to learn how to be content with the simpler things in life.

What past glories do you relive? Ask yourself when these glories occurred, what was the rest of your life like? Chances are the glories are associated with the relief of your emotional condition at the time. Today, whenever you experience those same emotions, that association takes you back to the glory, the achievement, and the money.

Sex and romance fantasies are no different. Over the years it was tempting, whenever I was lonely like that eleven-year-old boy, to go back to the picture of the smiling woman who seemed to relieve my pain. Have you ever gone back to your first romance, relived the excitement of that relationship, and wished you could find that person again? Remember that at the time of your first romance, you were probably unsure of yourself, awkward, and perhaps lonely. The adrenaline, dopamine, and the catecholamines we discussed in chapter 3 were at work in your mind back then. Your brain remembers that high and can return to it again and again. All of this produces thoughts that you would like to take captive.

A man named Doug came to one of our workshops because he had recently been arrested at the airport when a random bag search revealed he had pornographic pictures of teenage girls. Since they were underage and he was traveling across state lines, it was a felony. It is tempting to be judgmental and say, "How could a man have such disgusting pictures? Isn't he just a pervert, a dirty old man, and a sex offender?" As Paul Harvey would have said, "Here is the rest of the story."

Doug was sixteen years old when his parents got divorced. He lived in Minneapolis when his father left. His mother did not work and felt that she needed to move back to Iowa to live with her parents. Doug's grandparents were farmers and raised hogs. Now Doug found himself no longer living in a big city but on a farm. Grandpa had the old-fashioned idea that anyone living under his roof participated in the work of the farm, so at 4:30 every morning Doug found himself feeding hogs and cleaning out the pig pens. If this sounds familiar, check out Luke 15 and read the parable of the prodigal son. At his new, much smaller high school, the kids had all known each other since kindergarten and didn't accept Doug very well. As you can imagine, he missed his old friends and his dad and was generally miserable.

Grandma made everyone go to church, which is where Doug met a fifteen-year-old girl who took pity on him. They started a relationship, and one afternoon when they were all alone at her home in town, they both had sex for the first time. It was thrilling and Doug experienced a euphoria he had never known. It was a huge relief from the loneliness of his life. That was then. Now Doug lives in Minneapolis again, has plenty of friends, and a wonderful wife and children of his own. But whenever Doug was lonely or stressed, his thoughts returned to that magic moment and images of that girl. Eventually he went on the Internet to find pictures of girls that age. That led to downloading some of them, putting them in his briefcase, and his eventual arrest.

Would you still say Doug is perverted or a sex offender? Obviously his behavior is offensive to his family and those girls and he needs desperately to stop. Can you see, however, that this sinful act is the behavior of a terribly wounded man who learned long ago what could temporarily relieve his pain? Would we not be remiss if we didn't understand that pain and help him find healthier solutions? I guarantee you that if a community does help him with that, he will never offend again because he is simply a good man who did some bad things. Can you see that if we treat him as an offender, his behavior will probably get worse? The sexual fantasies were an old solution to an old pain. The pain of loneliness and isolation was caused by judgment and criticism, so to judge and criticize him now would only make things worse. Do you remember what Jesus did with the adulteress in John 8?

There is a happy ending to Doug's story. Doug took his thoughts and fantasies captive and made them obedient to Christ. He has restored his marriage and career. Today he is a model of what a broken and repentant man can be.

The story illustrates the principle I am trying to teach you: *old pain will equal old solution.* If the solution to old pain was a sexual thought or experience, that will be locked in the memory center of the brain until we can take it captive and find a healthier way to deal with it.

Here is one more story that illustrates my point. Michael was eleven when his ADD began making it hard for him to go to sleep at night. He would lie in bed wishing his mother would come in and comfort him, perhaps give him a back rub to calm him down (remember the powerful effect of touch and the oxytocin it produces in the brain). His mother, tired and stressed herself, never did come in, so Michael learned that he could create the desired effect by touching himself. He found that the place on his body that felt the best was his genitals. As he reached adolescence, the pattern of touching his genitals led to masturbation and he found that he just couldn't sleep without masturbating, which led him to look at pornography.

After he was married, Michael still had trouble sleeping. His wife, quite naturally, could not always provide sex at those times, so he would go downstairs and look at pornography on the Internet and then masturbate. One night, his wife, wondering where he was, went downstairs to check up on him and discovered the whole process. She was hurt and angry and had many questions about how this could be. Michael's marriage was in great jeopardy until he was able to take his thoughts captive, which involved understanding the old connection. Whenever his wife said no to sex, even though he knew at some level it was for normal reasons, at another level it triggered him to remember all those nights when his mother would never come in. That was the old pain, which led to the old solution.

Knowing all of this, Michael and his wife were able to learn more about healthy intimacy, and Michael discovered that there are much better solutions to the old pain. His wife was able to forgive him and marveled that because he was able to take his thoughts captive, he was also able to become the man and husband God called him to be.

● KEY POINT

There are three types of fantasies, all of which attempt to satisfy the desires of the soul:

1. They can replay a previous event with a different result.
2. They can bring what we think is the fulfillment of the desires of our soul.
3. They can replay a previous event that we interpreted as a relief to our loneliness, isolation, or stress.

● KEY QUESTIONS

The following are a short set of questions I use to help people capture the longings of their soul:

First, pick one of the fantasies (most of us have many) that you experience the most often. Allow yourself to interview it. Don't be afraid of it. In the past you've probably simply tried to tell it to go away. This time don't. Here are the questions.

1. Who are the people in your fantasy? What do they look like?

2. What do they do or say? How do they treat you?

3. Where does your fantasy happen? What is the scene or atmosphere like?

4. Finally, what happens or takes place? What is your behavior and what is the behavior of the other people like, if there are any other people?

I find that it is often helpful to write this down or journal your responses. You might say, "What?! Write this down? Are you crazy? Wouldn't that only invite me to be thinking about these sinful behaviors more? What if my spouse finds it?"

Let me assure you that the only way to get rid of your fantasies is to take them captive in this way. You will find that when you begin to understand them and find healthier solutions, they will no longer be messengers from your soul.

As for your spouse or friends finding out, what I am going to encourage you to do is to not share the specifics of your fantasy but to share the specifics of what you discover your soul really desires. If you are eventually able to do that, you will begin to experience an intimacy with your spouse or friends that will satisfy the desire of your soul.

Stay with me. This will take courage, but when you have captured your fantasies, turn to the next chapter and let's see if we can't make them obedient to Christ.

5

MAKING YOUR FANTASIES
OBEDIENT TO CHRIST

*Delight yourself in the LORD; and he will give you
the desires of your heart* (Ps. 37:4, NASB).

You have just answered some questions in chapter 4 that ought to have you really thinking about your fantasies, the very unwanted thoughts you're trying to get rid of. In chapter 1 I taught you some strategies for avoiding them, so you might be a little surprised that I have so openly asked you to think about them. Perhaps you're a little confused at the moment and a little worried that you have all of these thoughts in your head that you don't want there.

Remember that the strategies described in the first three chapters of this book are short-term approaches. Beginning with the previous chapter and continuing with this one and the next, I am trying to teach you long-term solutions. The first part of this book might be seen as combating a disease once you know the symptoms are there, while the second part of this book focuses on getting rid of the disease all together.

Now that you've taken your thoughts captive, what do you do with a captive? Some older cultures had a very good idea about all of this. For example, when Alexander the Great conquered and captured a group of people, it was assumed that they would be assimilated into Greek culture. They were taught the language, customs, philosophies, and beliefs of the Greeks. Gradually, wherever Alexander conquered you could find someone that spoke Greek and adhered to their culture and ideas.

This is why by the time of Christ and the New Testament there was a rather unified world to evangelize. Even Rome, the power of the day, had been greatly influenced by the Greeks. When Paul wrote to the Romans, Corinthians, Thessalonians, Philippians, or even Cretans (Titus), he was able to teach the gospel in a way that all these different people would understand. In the first chapter of John when he says that "the Word became flesh and made his dwelling among us" (v. 14), he is writing in Greek. The Greek word for "Word" is *logos*, a term that Greeks would understand refers to eternal truth.

The Roman principle of captivity was to capture something or someone and mold it to fit your beliefs, attitudes, and values. They realized that if you totally alienate a captured people, they will eventually rise up and rebel against you. If you, on the other hand, adopt them and instruct them in your ways, they become a part of you that will flow and cooperate with you.

This is why I believe it is important to embrace every unwanted thought and fantasy and shape them to fit your beliefs and values. If you simply tell them to go away, they will be rebellious and come back at you even stronger. Right now, for example, tell yourself to not think about your favorite food and see if you can. You might be trying to read this sentence but instead, the thought of that food is in your brain, is it not? So let me suggest this: embrace the thought of that food, tell it that it can stay, but that you will attend to eating it when you are sufficiently hungry and when it will have nutritional value for you. You might even tell the thought that it could be a reward for finishing this book!

The principle of capturing and embracing applies also to sinful thoughts and fantasies. People ask me since I have been successful in the area of sexual purity for almost twenty-five years if I ever have an inappropriate sexual thought or temptation. My answer usually surprises them because I say, "Of course I do; there are hundreds of sexual stimuli around me every day." You see, I haven't become a eunuch or stopped being a man. My strategy for capturing those sexual thoughts is threefold. First, I don't get angry at myself for having them. I don't beat myself up and feel guilty for having sexual temptations. God created us to be sexual beings and to "be fruitful, and multiply" (Gen. 1:28, KJV). To deny my sexuality would be against my human nature, so I no longer get freaked out when sexual thoughts enter my brain. I tell them that they can be there but I choose to not give them any energy and that I will certainly not act on them.

Second, I realize that my sexual energy is about creativity. There is a part of me that desires to be productive and to do so in a passionate way. I believe my sexual thoughts are harder to control when I'm not involved in productive and passionate activity and conversely, when I am involved in such activity, I am much less vulnerable to any kind of temptation. For those of you who have read my first book in this series on accountability, *The 7 Principles of Highly Accountable Men*, you might remember that Nehemiah principle number six is that we should be accountable to defend against attack and be building something in equal measure, fifty-fifty.

This second strategy can be applied to any fantasy or temptation. Let's say you have athletic fantasies. Could it be true that there is a part of you that desires to be active and energetic? If you have money fantasies, they could reflect a desire to be financially secure and to be responsible for money. Achievement fantasies have the same possibilities as the sexual fantasies because you desire to be creative, productive, and passionate. For those of you who have romantic fantasies or dream of the perfect person, might it not be true that you really desire deep intimacy with your friends or spouse?

Third, when I take my sexual fantasies captive, I ask them the questions I taught you in chapter 4. What do they mean? What is the lesson they are trying to teach me about what I truly desire? When I figure that out, I then ask myself how I'm going to get those desires met in healthy ways.

Did you answer the questions about fantasies I listed at the end of chapter 4? Let's go over them and try to understand

what some of the answers might mean. You may discover
that not all of these questions are as important as the others.
Maybe only one of them is really significant in your particular
fantasy.

1. Who are the people in your fantasy? What do they
   look like? This answer could be specific to body type,
   hair and eye color, height, and so forth. If you are able
   to identify a certain physical type of person, chances
   are that these characteristics are similar to a person in
   your past whom you feel didn't meet your needs. This
   means that this person is the one who abandoned you
   the most, and there has been a longing in your heart for
   the affirmations, blessings, love and nurturing, kindness,
   and listening ear of this person. Most often this person
   would be one of your parents, though this is not always
   the case.

   One of the dynamics we have noticed over the
   years, particularly with our sons and their friends, is
   how often their girlfriends or wives look like their mothers. This is only a part of the dynamic I'm talking about.
   When I ask men who frequently look at pornography
   what type of woman they find most stimulating, it is
   often either one that looks like their mother or their first
   love or sexual partner.

2. What do they do or say? How do they treat you? This
   answer usually has a lot to do with attitudes you wish
   others had and the words you long to hear. Remember
   when I wrote about that first woman staring at me from

the pages of a pornographic magazine? She was smiling and seemed to be looking at me as if she wanted me. In romance fantasies, the other person is interested in everything about you and he or she says and does all the right things. You should also know that when these fantasies lead to actual affairs, these behaviors are a part of what we call the infatuation stage of a relationship. During this stage, the other person is very purposefully doing all of these things.

In athletic, money, or achievement fantasies, the roar of the crowd, admiration of the public, or words of blessing from a spouse, boss, or friend are the attitudes and words you long to hear.

I have an exercise where I ask the men I work with to write a letter as if it was from their mom or dad. This letter should include all the words they have longed to hear. They may not know what those words are when they start, but they will when they are finished. It is amazing how they come pouring out once they start writing.

3. Where does your fantasy happen? What is the scene or atmosphere like? This question has the most to do with reliving past experiences, sometimes to imagine a different result and other times to re-create the feelings associated with that place and time. For instance, I can see the tennis court in Illinois where I played Jimmy Connors, I can remember the place where I first kissed my

wife, and I can see the place where one of my mentors first told me how proud he was of me.

You should be careful of this one because the sights, sounds, smells, feelings, and even the taste of things involved can all come flooding back. This can cause anxiety or be disconcerting if you don't know that it is normal for this kind of flashback to happen. It is simply a part of your brain trying to sort it out.

4. Finally, what happens or takes place? What is your behavior and what is the behavior of the other people like, if there are any other people? In these fantasies you win the game or lottery, get the award, achieve the position, or have sex or experience romance in ways that lift your spirit and allow you to feel positive emotions.

The answers to this question can be influenced by associations we have probably learned in our families and cultures. Some of these messages can be that

- Sex is equal to being loved.
- Money is equal to success.
- Athletic prowess is equal to being masculine, powerful, or equal to other men.
- Achievement is equal to blessing or acceptance.

There are many more possibilities. Many of us have been influenced by the messages of our mothers, fathers, schools, and churches. What did your dad value, for example? Mine valued education above all else. He also valued the ministry, so those are the things I dream about or strive toward in my life.

What does Hollywood project as happiness? Is it some infatuated form of love? Is it the next sexual encounter? Is it being so powerful we can survive any situation or take out any obstacle?

What about the church? Today is it teaching us that bigger is better? That the more members a church has, the more effective is the leadership? I know many pastors who become workaholics thinking that big is an indication they are superior pastors and, thereby, better Christians.

Let me say again that I have never heard a sexual act, however perverse, that doesn't have symbolic meaning. I want to write directly to the hearts of those reading this book who believe they have thought about or done sexual acts so despicable that not even God could love and forgive them. That simply is not true. Every sexual act symbolizes some form of excitement, acceptance, love, nurturing, power, or control; sexual acts are ways we symbolically try to solve our emotional issues. Your thoughts and actions mean something about your soul. Then know that "neither height nor depth, nor anything else in all creation, will be able to separate us from the love of God that is in Christ Jesus our Lord" (Rom. 8:39). Also know that you are not alone. However bizarre you think your thoughts are, someone else has thought them too. Paul says, "No temptation has seized you except what is common to man" (1 Cor. 10:13).

At one of our workshops was a man with a tremendous amount of shame because of the perceived "weirdness" of his fantasy. He was put in a small group with men from many other parts of the country. When he told his story, even I had not heard of that kind of activity before. Then the man next to him told his story and his fantasy was exactly the same as the first man. I believe that God somehow arranged for these two men from totally different places to be in that group at that time so that each one could know he was not alone. Their fantasy meant something, as different as it was, about what their hearts desired.

I pray that as I describe these dynamics, God is working with you through the power of the Holy Spirit. I pray that you will know that you are not alone and that your fantasies, whatever they are, mean something about the pain you are in and what your heart and soul truly desire. I trust that some awareness has come to you. Perhaps reading through this section has brought a great deal of sadness to you. If that is the case, know that you are on the right track. Your soul is wounded and longs to be healed. Others of you may be angry or anxious or both. Please know that these are the emotions of a person who has not received what he or she needs for a long time. Finally, others of you may have automatically thought of your fantasies. Embrace them and ask them to teach you about yourself.

● KEY POINT

Your fantasies and thoughts can be your teachers. They bring you messages from your soul.

● KEY QUESTIONS

- Can you be courageous enough to write down your most common fantasies?

- What stories from your youth have come to mind while reading this chapter?

- What were your answers to my four questions?

- What emotions came up while reading this chapter?

- Would you be willing to talk to someone about what you've learned?

What Does Obedience Really Mean?

One of the problems with knowing how to take thoughts captive and make them obedient comes from your idea of obedience. We all tend to think about obedience as keeping black-and-white rules that are not to be broken. When it comes to fantasies and unwanted thoughts, we tend to think that obedience is not having them in the first place or getting rid of them quickly when they do happen.

Jesus was very clear about all of this. I believe that the key to obedience was his teaching about law. In a running dialogue with the scribes and Pharisees, hear how Jesus responds to a question about law:

> One of them, an expert in the law, tested him with this question: "Teacher, which is the greatest commandment in the Law?" Jesus replied: "'Love the Lord your God with all your heart and with all your soul and with all your mind.' This is the first and greatest commandment. And the second is like it: 'Love your neighbor as yourself.' All the Law and the Prophets hang on these two commandments." (Matt. 22:35-40)

Focus with me on the truth here. We are to love God with all of our heart, soul, and mind. That covers all the thoughts and fantasies we have been talking about. Loving God is the way to put positive thoughts in our brain. Then Jesus says something rather interesting when he tells us to love our neighbors as we love ourselves. This is a central teaching of the gospel. Jesus says it another way in Luke 6:31: "Do to others as you would have them do to you."

We might begin by understanding that our thoughts and fantasies are an offense against others. How would we feel, for instance, if others had those same thoughts and fantasies that were an offense against us? For example, if a man fantasizes about having an affair, how would he feel if his wife was doing the same thing? According to Jesus, we need to think thoughts about others that we would have them think about us.

That is a good place to start to practice what Jesus is teaching us. To me, however, the key to understanding obedience for our purposes is found in one short word of Jesus' commandment: "Love your neighbor *as* yourself" (Matt. 22:39, emphasis added). The Greek word for "as" here is *hos*, which is translated in other parts of the Bible as the words "how," "even as," "as soon as," and "after." The gist of all these is the same: we can only love others in the same way, as soon as, after, how, and as we love ourselves. In short, *loving ourselves comes first*, then we love others. To be obedient to Christ's commandment, then, we must learn to love ourselves.

Isn't that consistent with what God wants us to know? God loves us. Yet we do not always know or understand that. Our fantasies are our attempts to love ourselves, to meet the needs of our soul. God's love for us has been the answer all along, but do we know how that works? The psalmist says that if we "delight . . . in the LORD . . . he will give [us] the desires of [our] heart" (Ps. 37:4). Could it be that being obedient to Christ means that we'd better learn how God loves us and wants us to love ourselves so that we can love others? If God wants us to love ourselves and it is that important to loving others, maybe we better get over the idea that doing so might be selfish. It might, on the other hand, be the key to being selfless.

As always, some examples might help. I'll start with an extreme example that I encountered recently that so vividly illustrates my point. David struggled with same-sex attraction and fantasized about a certain sexual activity with men. He wanted to stop doing that and to love his wife in the ways he knew God wanted him to do. This fantasy had become especially vivid right after his father died. In his youth, David's father had been emotionally absent and often physically absent. Now

David's father is permanently absent. I told him that I thought his fantasies about men who always looked like his father were trying to tell him that he missed what a father should give to a son. I also told him that I thought the sexual acts he thought about were simply symbolic ways in which he felt loved, accepted, and nurtured.

Since his father is gone, David now faces the challenge to love himself. He can do that by accepting the love of two different kinds of fathers. First is David's heavenly Father, God. David was struggling to accept God's fatherly love for him because his soul was very wounded by his own father. The second type of fathers in his life were a group of older men that he really looked up to and thought were great models. I asked him if he would be willing to love himself by asking these men to spend time with him. Nothing big, just going out for coffee or a meal, having a conversation after church, or engaging in some activity together. With my constant encouragement, David started doing that. This took place over several months, and today, David is free of his fantasies; he doesn't need them as messengers anymore because he has accepted God's fatherly love and a group of older men have become surrogate fathers to him.

David may very well struggle with same-sex attraction and temptations again in his life. Each time, however, he now knows that it signals a longing in his soul for a relationship with a man. If he loves himself by allowing himself to have healthy relationships with men, then it will free him up to love others, including his wife.

In a similar way, Kathy had romantic fantasies about men. She read at least one romance novel a week and was hooked on several soap operas. There were several fairly famous men that she thought about all the time and lately she had been going online and meeting men on social networking sites. Kathy's therapist was quick to explore the relationship she had with her father. "Oh, he was a drunk," she said. "Thank God he was never home because when he was, he was always angry." Where are Kathy's fantasies coming from? She, like David, was looking for the kindness, affirmation, love, nurturing, and blessing from a man. Kathy's therapist encouraged her to invite her husband to therapy, and together they worked on greater intimacy. As Kathy and her husband have been getting emotionally and spiritually closer, her fantasies have been disappearing.

Chuck grew up in a family of eight kids. Neither of his parents had much time for any of the kids, so he had missed the blessing from both his mom and dad. In his adult life, Chuck fantasized about the next promotion and worked constantly to get his bosses' approval. He also spent time at work looking at pornography. He was longing for that blessing he never received from his parents and thought it would come in the form of a promotion. He also found the love and nurturing he had missed out on from the women in pornography.

I asked Chuck what he really liked to do. He said he had always wanted to write. I encouraged him to attend a writing class and see what happened. Today he has published several short pieces and, rather than work all the time, spends a great deal of his recreation time writing. Chuck has also learned to find not only affirmation and kindness from men in a Bible study he participates in but also the accountability to stop watching porn. Chuck has invited his wife to a spiritual retreat where they renewed their marriage vows. He is very attentive every day to check in with his wife, spends time in Bible study with her, and has generally learned how to enjoy the relationship.

As I'm writing this, I realize that I could fill a whole book, much longer than this, just with examples of what I'm trying to teach. I hope these short case studies are getting you to think for yourself. In summary, here are the steps I've been outlining that will allow you to take your thoughts captive and make them obedient:

● KEY POINT

1. Understand that your thoughts and fantasies are messages from your soul.
2. Take time to know what the longings of your soul are and where in your past they come from.
3. Learn how to love yourself by getting the longings and desires of your soul fulfilled in godly ways.
4. Your fantasies and unwanted thoughts will disappear because you no longer need them as messengers. You will then be free to love others.

● KEY QUESTIONS

Today, I know that whenever I start to fantasize about anything or when unwanted thoughts come into my brain, my first question is going to be, "What are these thoughts trying to tell me? What are they trying to teach me?" I don't tell them to go away. I ask them to stay, and I interview them. Then I ask myself, "Am I particularly tired or lonely? Am I stressed and overworked? Am I feeling disconnected from my wife, family, and friends?" Then, "What do I need? How can I love myself? What do I need to ask for?" When I take time to do this, I can honestly say that I am free of unwanted thoughts and fantasies and am much more able to love others.

God is good. He is the answer. I seek to be obedient, and I seek to love others as I love myself. Do you?

In the final chapter, I have one last idea about taking thoughts captive: we can do so by exchanging our fantasies and thoughts for vision.

6
CREATING VISION

Where there is no vision, the people perish: but he that keepeth the law, happy is he (Prov. 29:18, KJV).

In the previous two chapters, one of the teaching principles I have been trying to get across is that fantasies are often misguided expression of our desire to be intimate, productive, creative, and passionate. One of the ways to correct that would be to find healthy Christ-centered, Christ-obedient ways to express those desires. In my first book in this series, *The 7 Principles of Highly Accountable Men,* I explained that one of the ways to be accountable is to build and to be productive.

I would suggest that the main way to be productive, passionate, and creative is to participate in God's calling in our life. The way I believe we do that is by understanding a true and godly vision for our lives.[10] If we know what that is, we can replace our fantasies with vision. Vision will then preoccupy the mental images in our brain, literally driving out the unwanted thoughts. One of the ways, therefore, to take our thoughts captive and to make them obedient to Christ is to make them obedient to God's calling in our lives.

The Bible is often very clear that we should put healthy and positive thoughts in our mind. My favorite place is Paul's command in Philippians when he says,

> Finally, brothers, whatever is true, whatever is noble, whatever is right, whatever is pure, whatever is lovely, whatever is admirable—if anything is excellent or praiseworthy—think about such things. Whatever you have learned or received or heard from me, or seen in me—put it into practice. And the God of peace will be with you. (4:8-9)

Some preachers, like Norman Vincent Peale and Robert Schuller, have made a sermonic career in preaching about positive thinking. The important principle, which most psychologists would also confirm, is that whatever we put in our mind or our brain will drive everything we see and do.

In that great book of wisdom, the writer of Proverbs says that if we as a people don't have a "vision," we will "perish" (Prov. 29:18, KJV). Vision is important because it drives our lives. As Christians, that vision should be from God. When we seek to understand what vision is, we should first understand the power that mental images have to drive our life.

Mental Images Drive Our Behaviors

To start, here is a simple example. Several years ago I needed a new car. These days you can effectively shop online, but eventually you will need to go to a dealership and test-drive one. I wanted an SUV with all-wheel drive because I like to sit up high and I like the traction during Minnesota winters. I also wanted my new car to be fuel efficient. With SUVs, those criteria don't always go together. I discovered, however, that several car companies are now making more efficient cars, including hybrids. So I looked and finally decided to drive several, eventually picking the one I really wanted. It met all my criteria, including being a hybrid. Now I had a mental picture of the car I was going to buy. From that point on, I began to see every car of that type on the road. It was truly amazing how many people drove the car I wanted. You see, my mental picture of what I wanted affected what I saw out in the world.

Michelangelo once said, "Everything is created twice, first in the mind, and then in reality." He knew, even artistically, that you must first see in your brain what you want and then it will become reality. When I began writing a book, one of my mentors told me to visualize the cover of the book in my mind. That advice helped me later when the publisher sent me the cover design long before I had actually written the book. Before my sobriety, one of my early addiction sponsors or accountability partners told me to imagine myself at a twelve-step meeting where I was to receive congratulations for my first year of sobriety. We are driven by what we see, and sometimes, what we see can be created first in our imagination.

This principle can also be not so positive, however. According to Scripture, Satan is capable of using images to tempt us. Before Jesus officially began his ministry, he went out in the desert. There Satan came to him with various temptations. For his last temptation, "the devil took him to a very high mountain and showed him all the kingdoms of the world and their splendor. 'All this I will give you,' he said, 'if you will bow down and worship me'" (Matt. 4:8-9). Notice that he showed Jesus images of all the great kingdoms on earth. We know the result of that confrontation and benefit from the fact that Jesus chose a different vision.

We are not often that strong. A person who thinks of having the next sexual encounter will notice more of the type of person he or she is attracted to. A person who has been looking at pornography will undress with the eyes many of the people he or she encounters during an average day. Someone who compulsively gambles will notice every sign for the nearest casino when driving. A person who compulsively eats will sit down to dinner and not be able to turn down any food. They also are terrible shoppers because when they see the food in the store, they will be unable to resist and will consequently buy too much food. A man or woman who dreams of achieving at all costs will stay at work longer because he or she can't help seeing the next task that "needs" to get done.

Let's reverse this last list. Suppose the person who envisions the next affair would mentally visualize an image of his or her spouse more often. The man who looks at pornography might put the images of his own daughters or other young girls he really cares about in his brain. The gambler might put the image of his or her bank statement completely in the black in his or her mind. The food addict can put pictures on the refrigerator of himself or herself when he or she was thin or pictures of very fit people. The workaholic might visualize in the mind pictures of his or her family or imagine family times together. These images are consistent with the vision God has called these people to see.

● KEY POINT

Mental pictures drive everything we see in the world, which determines what we do. What we do can either be for the glory of God or for sinful purposes. Try this: pick up the newspaper, a magazine, or watch TV. Pick out an advertisement for some product and then keep track of how many times you think of or see that product over the next few days.

How Do We Know What God Wants Us to See?

I believe that you will know what God wants you to see by testing it against reality and your own intuition. If your picture is not a true vision, God will correct it. Over six years ago, my wife and I were renting space for our counseling center. I was getting frustrated with paying rent and all the control the landlord exerted, so I began to get a picture in my mind of what the ideal counseling center would look like. My original picture was very large. Since we live in Minnesota, I got an "up-north" picture in my brain. I saw a ten-thousand-square-foot building, all constructed of logs and timbers, with lots of fireplaces and many other rustic features. It had counseling rooms, group rooms, and sleeping quarters for the people who come to our workshops. The building sat on many acres and included its own lake. There was a horse barn for equine therapy or at least relaxation. What a great picture.

We soon found out about reality. Land, as I imagined, that was close to us cost millions of dollars, and so did the construction. Horses are expensive to maintain. Undaunted, Debbie and I went to the Minneapolis Log and Timber Frame

Show at the Minneapolis Convention Center. We approached a number of builders whose first question was always, "Where is your land?" We didn't have any nor did we have millions of dollars. I was very discouraged when one day I was driving home from our rented center and saw a sign for a builder who was constructing build-to-suit town-home-like office buildings. I called the builder and found out that his next project was on a beautiful piece of land with a small pond in the back that was just two miles from our house. I was excited, but he said he had presold all of the units. He asked what I wanted to do with one, so I told him we were a Christian counseling ministry that brought men and couples into our center from all over the country to heal from sexual sin and infidelity. The next day, this builder, who was a Christian, called me and said he was moved by our vision and would sell us the unit he had reserved for himself.

Next came the all-important question, "How much is it?" Well, it wasn't several millions or even a million dollars, but I certainly didn't know how to pay for it. I shared the possibility with a friend of mine who used to work for Walt Disney World and was instrumental in opening some of the other Disney theme parks. He was a man of big pictures. When I told him how much it was, he said, "So what is the big deal with that?" To him, it was a drop in the bucket, while to us it was a fortune. This wonderful Christian man patiently walked us through how to get the right financing. Today, our counseling center sits in a complex of units. Our back windows face a pond with many pine trees. We designed the space with several fireplaces and put faux timber beams in the ceilings of our group room. What we have is more than enough, and to date, more than one thousand people have come to us for help at that building.

Here's the deal. I had a picture that was part vision and part fantasy. God, through the practical realities of the situation, corrected the fantasy and brought it down to realistic size. Then, in my faith, he brought two fine Christian men into the picture who made it happen. I should also say that God provided me with a wife of immense financial skill who was also instrumental in making the financing manageable.

⊛ KEY POINT

Start with a picture you believe is in line with your calling in life. If it is a fantasy, God will correct it. When it is a vision, God will bring people into your life who will help.

A Vision Is Consistent with Calling

You may be wondering how you know what is consistent with your calling. My answer is simple; you will know your calling when you feel moved in your soul and experience passion. I'm not talking about sinful passion; I'm talking about spiritual passion.

Here is one last story from my own life. A few years ago, Debbie dragged me to the Willow Creek Church Leadership Conference. I went somewhat reluctantly and wondered in my sarcastic mind where the "Follower's Conference" was because not everyone can be a leader. I was impressed, however, when we accidentally sat in back of the then governor of our state,

Tim Pawlenty, and his wife. I said to myself, "If the governor of our state can sit here in a regular seat, then maybe I can too."

And I was inspired. On the last day, the pastor of Willow Creek, Bill Hybels, challenged the entire gathering by asking how many of us were descendants of the Europeans who first brought Christianity to America. Many of us raised our hands. He then said that today only about 2 percent of the European population even goes to church. "Maybe it's time for some of us descendants to take Christianity back over there," he said. For some reason, I felt stirred and thought, "Yes, here am I, Lord, send me." I was actually moved to tears. But then I remembered I am not an evangelist. I felt stuck but then was nudged in my spirit by this question, "What is it you do again?" The words of my wife and my vision statement came instantly into my mind. Our vision as a couple has been "to preach, teach, write, and counsel for the purpose of educating the church about sexual purity." Everything we have done since we started working together in ministry has been directed by that vision.

Then there was another question in my mind, "Where are you from again?" My ancestors are from Germany. There was a follow-up question: "Do you think there are any Germans who are not sexually pure?" I pictured the red-light districts in many German cities. I also remembered the biblical truth that the sins of the father can be passed down (see Lev. 26:39). "Okay, God, I get it; some of my ancestors must have had sexual purity issues as I do. So what do you want me to do about it?" Well, the answer was clear: go to Germany and educate German psychologists, pastors, and counselors about sexual purity.

Now I had the picture, one of me standing in front of a German audience and lecturing. There was one problem: I didn't have any invitations to go there, much less did I know any Christian counselors in Germany who might help.

The next week I was having breakfast with Dr. Archibald Hart, one of the wise, older male mentors in my life, at the world's largest hotel, the Gaylord Opryland in Nashville. We were surrounded by thousands of Christian counselors from all over the world. I knew Arch traveled, so I was asking him about his latest events and he returned the question. So I shared my vision.

Arch listened and then sat silently for a short while before he said, "Do you see that man sitting at the table next to us? That is Dr. Ulrich Giesekus and he is a German psychologist who puts on seminars in Germany. Would you like to meet him?" So we invited ourselves to *frühstück* (breakfast in German) where Ulrich got excited by the vision. One year later I was in Germany doing a series of seminars for exactly the audience that God had called me to speak to. It was a wonderful trip.

⊛ KEY POINT

Be careful what you visualize in your brain. You must decide if Satan or God put it there. My advice is to share it with other Christians who will help you sort out calling from fantasy. They might just be the ones who will help you to pull it off, as in my two examples.

✸ KEY QUESTIONS

- What pictures are in your brain?

- What are you doing when you feel passionate?

- Do you have a vision statement for your calling, plan, and purpose in life?

- If you are married, have you ever shared that with your wife?

- Have you ever shared it with anyone?

One very important part of this set of questions is whether or not you have shared a vision with your spouse. So often I encounter couples where each member might have a vision, but they have never shared it with each other. This creates two visions that might draw a couple apart. Put another way, two visions not shared equals *division*.

I like to think in terms of formulas sometimes. In summary, let me put this whole chapter to you this way:

**Fantasy = mental pictures of what you think
will meet your desires**

↓

These pictures will create an appetite for what you see.
↓
**That appetite will determine everything
you see in the world.**
↓
What you see will determine all of your behaviors.

On the other hand:

Vision = God's picture based on your calling
↓
**This picture will create in you a hunger
and thirst for righteousness.**
↓
**This hunger will determine everything
you see in the world.**
↓
What you see will determine all of your behaviors.

My prayer for you is that God will give you a mighty vision and that in so doing you will see his exact plan and purpose for your life. When this hunger and thirst is in your mind and heart, I pray that it will direct everything you see and do. In this way, your battle to take every thought captive will be totally subject to God's desires and totally obedient to Christ's commandment that you love others as you love yourself.

CONCLUSION

An author reaches a point, I think, in which he feels that he has said everything he wants to say on a certain topic. I have the satisfying feeling that I have done so in this book. My final words to you are ones of encouragement.

My guess is that you picked up or were referred to this book because you have had trouble taking thoughts captive. You have had no idea how to make those thoughts obedient to Christ. Perhaps you have felt a lot of discouragement and shame about that. Perhaps there are others, like your spouse, who are also angry or discouraged with you. Maybe they are even threatening to leave.

Be of good courage. I have one last suggestion that is a restatement of a truth I have mentioned throughout this book. If you are at all encouraged by this book, find a friend to hold you accountable to answering all the questions in this book. Share your answers with at least one other person. Ask that person to encourage you to put into practice the principles contained here. Start with chapter 1 and the most immediate strategies to help you avoid sinful thoughts and fantasies. Then ask your accountability partner(s) to remind you to meditate, study God's Word, and pray. If you think your brain has been holding you back, get that checked out medically and then put into practice one or more of the strategies listed in chapter 3.

When you have done this and have hopefully begun to gain some victory over your thoughts, dive into the last three chapters. These are difficult chapters to digest and incorporate into your life alone. Fellowship with other Christian men or women will always be the key to becoming the man or woman you want to become.

Finally, may God truly convince you of his love for you and that no matter what you've done or thought, he has not only forgiven it through the gift of his Son, Jesus, but also forgotten it. May he then also give you a vision of the man or woman he calls you to be.

In this way, may your thoughts always be captured, may they always be your teachers about what you truly desire, and may you find ways to love yourself and then be able to love others.

NOTES

1. Hamilton B., *Getting Started in AA* (Center City, Minn.: Hazelden, 1995), 117.

2. *Wikipedia,* s.v. "Where Everybody Knows Your Name," http://en.wikipedia.org/wiki/Where_Everybody_Knows_Your_Name (accessed May 26, 2011).

3. Mark R. Laaser, *The 7 Principles of Highly Accountable Men* (Kansas City: Beacon Hill Press of Kansas City, 2011).

4. Daniel Amen, *Change Your Brain, Change Your Life* (New York: Three Rivers Press, 1998).

5. AACC can be found on the Web at www.AACC.net or by calling them at 1-800-526-8673.

6. For good summaries of this, check out www.webMD.com or www.Mayoclinic.com and put exercise and depression in the search bar.

7. The study was published April 4, 2006, in the *International Journal of Psychiatry in Medicine.*

8. William Struthers, *Wired for Intimacy* (Wheaton, Ill.: Navigators Press, 2010).

9. Any names that I use in reference to the lives of people are fictitious.

10. Most of what I have to teach in this chapter was greatly influenced and shaped by my colleague and friend Eli Machen. Eli is a brilliant preacher and teacher. Even though he has never published his teaching on vision, I hope that this chapter will give him a sense of pleasure that his wisdom might be positively influencing others.

RESOURCES

One of the dynamics I have observed over the years is how often contact information, Web sites, and the availability of books change. We are living in an electronic age and so much of what we read is on the Internet. So rather than list books or articles that I find helpful, I encourage you to stay in touch with the most recent material by regularly checking Web sites or doing Internet searches for information relevant to your needs.

There are two Web sites that will most likely continue to be current:

1. Our Web site is www.faithfulandtrueministries.com. On it you will find articles, videos, references to helpful books, and other counseling resources. A calendar of our workshops and speaking engagements throughout the country are included as well. We also provide, without charge, general education to the public through Web-based seminars, or Webinars. We will likewise be offering training Webinars for professionals, such as pastors and counselors, with the possibility, in some cases, of participants earning CEUs. Lectures by Debbie, other colleagues, and myself will also be archived on this site. Material from this book series will at times be presented as well.

2. Another Web site is www.aacc.net. This is the site of the American Association of Christian Counseling. The AACC is the largest association of Christian counselors in the world. This site has a directory of counselors in your area. You will also find on this site several video training series on a number of topics. It is possible to get trained as a lay counselor or certified in several areas as a professional counselor by using these video courses. Some of those video series include Debbie and me. The AACC also conducts large national and international conferences that are a joy to attend. It is the best place to network with colleagues and friends. So stay in touch with what they are doing.

When lost in the maze of the Web, please call or email us directly. I, Debbie, or one of our staff will get back to you with specific questions. We enjoy pointing people in the right direction.

Mark R. Laaser, MDiv, PhD

Debbie Laaser, MA

Faithful and True Ministries, Inc.

15798 Venture Lane

Eden Prairie, MN 55344

952-746-3880

mlaaser@faithfulandtrueministries.com

dlaaser@faithfulandtrueministries.com

www.faithfulandtrueministries.com

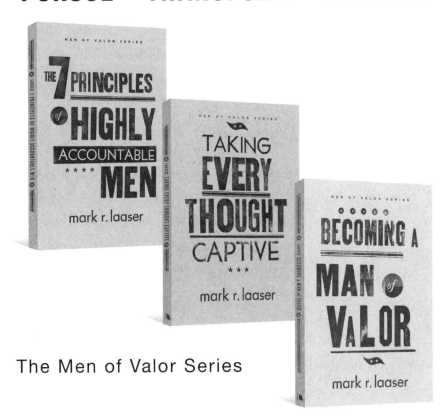